ISBN: 9781313465830

Published by:
HardPress Publishing
8345 NW 66TH ST #2561
MIAMI FL 33166-2626

Email: info@hardpress.net
Web: http://www.hardpress.net

PR
9599
L42A
1917

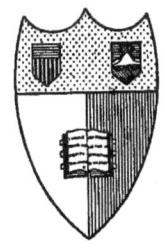

Cornell University Library
Ithaca, New York

BOUGHT WITH THE INCOME OF THE
SAGE ENDOWMENT FUND
THE GIFT OF
HENRY W. SAGE
1891

The date shows when this volume was taken.
To renew this book copy the call No. and give to the librarian.

HOME USE RULES

All Books subject to recall

All borrowers must register in the library to borrow books for home use.

All books must be returned at end of college year for inspection and repairs.

Limited books must be returned within the four week limit and not renewed.

Students must return all books before leaving town. Officers should arrange for the return of books wanted during their absence from town.

Volumes of periodicals and of pamphlets are held in the library as much as possible. For special purposes they are given out for a limited time

Borrowers should not use their library privileges for the benefit of other persons.

Books of special value and gift books, when the giver wishes it, are not allowed to circulate.

Readers are asked to report all cases of books marked or mutilated.

Do not deface books by marks and writing.

Cornell University Library
PR 9599.L42A6 1918

Selected poems;

3 1924 013 249 515

SELECTED POEMS OF HENRY LAWSON

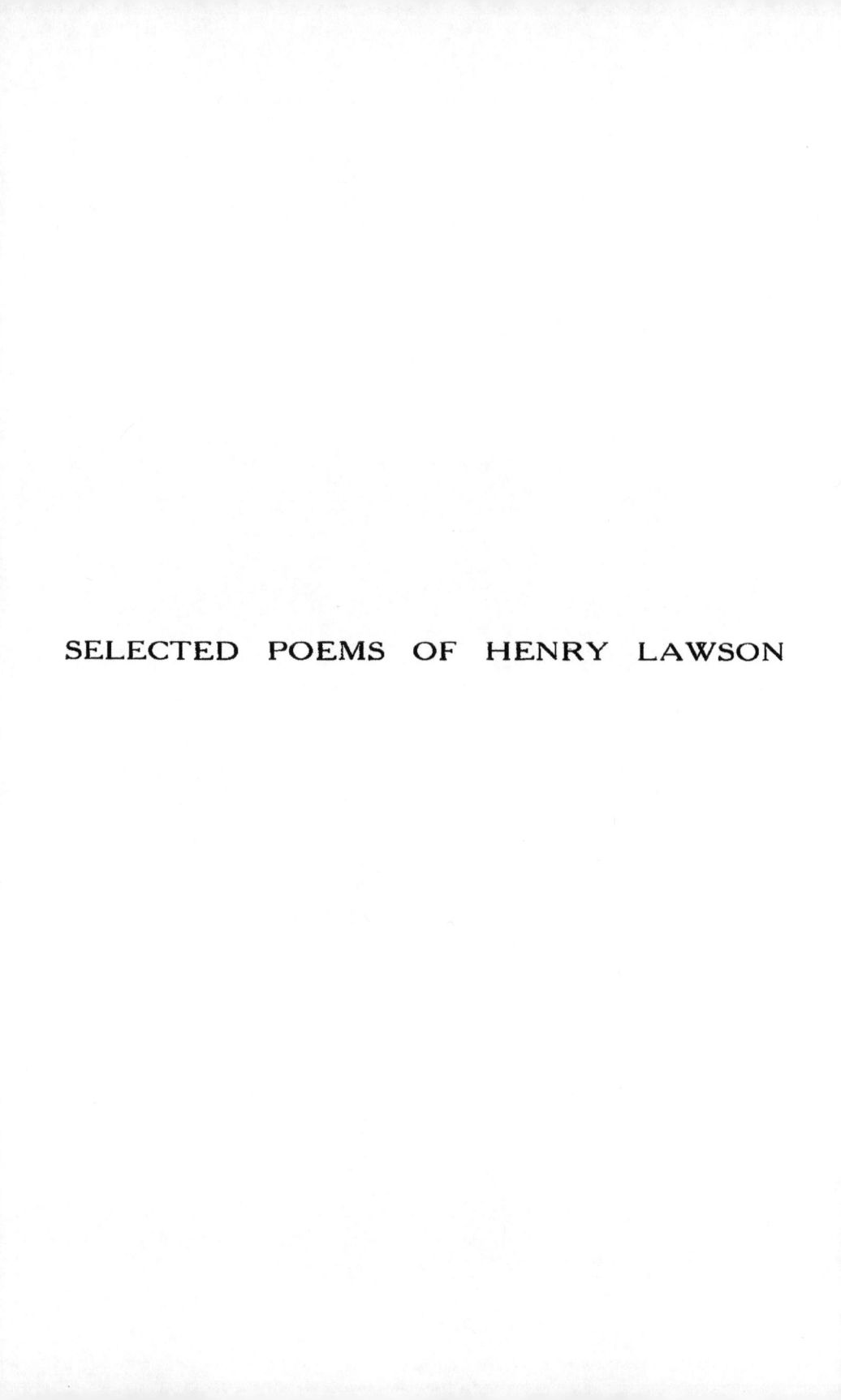

"Above Crow's Nest" is included by permission of the Lothian Book Publishing Co Pty Ltd, and *"My Army, O My Army"* by that of Messrs Tyrrell's Ltd.

The other poems, including several reprinted from THE BULLETIN and THE LONE HAND, which now appear for the first time in book form, and all the alterations in the older pieces, are copyrighted, 1918, by Angus & Robertson Ltd.

This edition consists of 2000 copies. The engravings are by Messrs Bacon & Co Ltd; the printing and binding by Messrs W. C. Penfold & Co Ltd.

Henry Lawson
From the portrait by John Longstaff in the National Gallery, Sydney

Selected Poems of Henry Lawson

Illustrated by Percy Leason

Sydney
Angus and Robertson Ltd
Publishers to the University
1918

A 464197

TO GEORGE ROBERTSON

PREFACE

WHEN James Cook lifted the veil that had long masked the Terra Incognita of the south, a fresh breeze of adventure blew across the souls of Englishmen. Here for conquest were virgin lands—lands with no history, no legend of achievement or shame—and needing for their conquest no sword, but only strong hearts and an enduring purpose. Men might have seen in their dreams a wider, sweeter England rising as by magic over far oceans, free of fettering old-world traditions, a source of light and leading to all. To claim that such a vision has been realized would be as yet too much; but the foundations have been laid. The wide spaces of the Australian continent are developing a race British in fibre and texture, yet unlike the peoples of Britain in every mere external. It is hard to discern the heights to which this race may attain in the brave days yet to be; but a nation in the making is always an object of supreme interest. Processes that in the days of the Heptarchy moulded Kent and Yorkshire are even now moulding Tasmania and

Queensland. It was inevitable that such a race in the making, such a land in the shaping, should find its singer; and that, the singer found, his music should be different from that of all others.

Henry Lawson is the first articulate voice of the real Australia. Other singers in plenty the southern continent knows and has known—men and women following bravely in the broad pathway where Byron strode and Wordsworth loitered; but one alone has found the heart of the new land, its rugged strength, its impatience of old restraints, its hopes and fears and despairs, its irreverence and grim humour, and the tenderness and courage that underlie them all. Lawson is never exquisite as are our greater lyrists. The axemarks show in his work everywhere. But he is sincere and strong and true; and the living beauty in that sincerity and strength and truth grips us more than any delicate craftsmanship. His laughter is as genuine as that of the wind and the sea; he weeps as Australians of the bush weep, with dry eyes and a hard curving mouth. He knows men and women—his men and women. In the world's loneliest places he has grasped hard hands alive with heroic meaning; in crowded cities, where the shames of older nations have overflowed into the new, he has felt the throb of emotions too fine for civilization's sordid setting. In Lawson, too, there is a splendid scorn—the scorn of the Things-that-Are—and always as he looks into the eyes of his world, seeking the best in the worst, his indignation blazes against the shams and the shows that have been brought across the seas to hold Liberty from her purpose. Lawson has lived his people's life, seen with their eyes, felt throb for throb with them in pain and joy; and he sets it all to a rugged music of his own that goes straight to the heart.

PREFACE

When in April, 1915, Australians made the historic landing at Gaba Tepe, the unexpectant world saw young soldiers from a peaceful Commonwealth bearing themselves in the stress of war like veterans of the older fighting nations. The spectacle arrested and surprised. But Lawson had sung of these things more than twenty years before. Nothing that Australians did in Gallipoli, or later in the fields of France, was new or strange to those who remembered the bugle note of his early poems. With prophetic insight he had dreamed a people's dream—had felt in that soldier-heart of his early manhood the tremor of a coming tempest, though the world skies were then clear—and had foreknown with every fibre of his being the way in which men of the bush and the mountain and plain would respond to the battle-call.

What of the man who has done and felt these things? He lives his life in Australia still—a life very close to ours, yet remote and lonely as that of genius is wont to be. London called to him, and he left us for a while, but came back more Australian than when he went away. You meet him in the street and are arrested by his eyes. Are there such eyes anywhere else under such a forehead? He has the softened speech of the deaf, but the eyes speak always more than the voice; and the grasp of his hand is brotherly. A sense of great sympathy and human kindliness is always about him. You will not talk much with Lawson, but you will not lightly forget your first meeting. A child will understand him better than a busy city man, for the child understands the eternal language of the heart written in the eye; and Australia, strong-thewed pioneer though she be, has enough of the child left in her to understand her son.

Henry Lawson was born in a tent on the Grenfell goldfield in

1867. His father was a Norse sailor who became a digger; his mother came of a Kentish family of gipsy blood and tradition. Henry spent his boyhood on old mining fields, and on a selection his father had taken up. Later, he came to Sydney and learned coachpainting, attended a night school, dabbled in spiritualism, and was caught in the wave of socialism. Very early his verses attracted attention. He was the voice of a new movement; the ringing, surging rebellion of his song echoed the unrest of the eighties and nineties, years full of great labour strikes and the breaking up of old political parties. Then he wandered far into the interior of Australia—his fame growing all the while—saw and shared the rude strenuous life of his brothers in a dozen varieties of toil, crossed over to New Zealand, and added to the tang of the gum leaves something of the salt of the great Southern Ocean. He has lived the life that he sings and seen the places of which he writes; there is not a word in all his work which is not instantly recognized by his readers as honest Australian. The drover, the stockman, the shearer, the rider far on the skyline, the girl waiting at the sliprails, the big bush funeral, the coach with flashing lamps passing at night along the ranges, the man to whom home is a bitter memory and his future a long despair, the troops marching to the beat of the drum, the coasting vessel struggling through blinding south-westerly gales, the great grey plain, the wilderness of the Never-Never—in long procession the pictures pass, and every picture is a true one because Henry Lawson has been there to see with the eyes of his heart.

At twenty-one, Lawson was probably the most remarkable writer of verse in Australia. Some critics of those days thought his genius prematurely developed, and likely to flame up strongly *and fade away swiftly. Lawson disappointed their predictions. He remained; he continued to write; he gathered grip and force as the years went by. The dates of original publication attached to each poem in this collection will enable the reader to follow the author's progress. They cover a wide range of years. Before he had reached his twenty-first birthday, Lawson, keenly alive to all the movements about him in Sydney, found one political faction discussing a closer imperialism of a rather mechanical pattern, while another cried for an equally machine-made socialism. He listened to the outpourings of oratory one night, and, remembering the growth of wealth and luxury on the one hand and the increasing squalor of the city slums on the other, went home and wrote* FACES IN THE STREET—*a notable achievement that brought him immediate local fame. Seven years afterwards, still with the passionate hope of a purifying revolution in his heart, he saw* THE STAR OF AUSTRALASIA *rise through tumult and battle smoke and foretold, in lines that surge and sweep, the storm that was to break down divisions between rich and poor, and to call to life a great nationhood through a baptism of blood. At forty-eight he sang of* MY ARMY, O MY ARMY, *the struggling "Vanguard" always suffering in the trenches of civilization that others might go on to victory. Never was the view of the final triumph obscured; but the means by which it might be attained seemed more clouded in doubt as the years went by. Then, when he had completed his full half-century of life, the poet's vision cleared. At fifty he wrote* ENGLAND YET, *a song of pride in a greater nationality, wider and more embracing than the old Australia of his dreams. Here is natural progression of thought—a mind growing with the years, a hope enlarging with the great movements of the race.*

In simpler and homelier themes the continual widening of his sympathy is equally marked. THE DROVER'S SWEETHEART, *with its sob of delight in the last stanza, was written at twenty-two. Ten years afterwards he penned the tenderest and most perfect of all his poems,* THE SLIPRAILS AND THE SPUR. *Dear old* BLACK BONNET—*a picture as true as it is sweet in all years and all places—first tripped to church in his verse when he was forty-nine; at fifty,* SCOTS OF THE RIVERINA *showed that he had not lost his power of dealing with the tragedy that underlies life's commonplace. The reader may trace a similar growth of sympathy for the men and women whom civilization condemns, or who have come to be regarded as "down and out." He saw* SWEENEY *with battered humorous face and empty bottle in 1891;* PAST CARIN', *with its completeness of heartbreak, was written in 1899; and the grim realism of* ONE-HUNDRED-AND-THREE, *which must stand among Lawson's greatest efforts, appeared in 1908. Always there is growth, apparent from year to year and decade to decade. The verses vary greatly in merit and manner, but the thought and feeling behind them move on into wider places. Lawson fulfilled his first promise and did something more.*

Of Lawson's place in literature it is idle to speak. Something of what Burns did for Scotland, something of what Kipling did for India, he has done for Australia; but he is not in the least like either Kipling or Burns. Judged as verse, his work has nearly always a certain crudity; judged by the higher standard of poetry, it is often greatest when the crudity is most apparent. In the coming chances and changes it is daring to predict immortality for any writer. The world is being remade in fire and pain; in that remaking every standard of achievement may be altered utterly from those to which we have been accustomed;

but if permanency is to be looked for anywhere, it is in vital, red-blooded work such as Lawson's—work that came so straight from the heart that it must always find a heart to respond to it. All Australia is there, painted with a big brush in the colours in which its people see it.

David McKee Wright.

September, 1918.

CONTENTS

	PAGE
England Yet	1
The Star of Australasia	3
The Sliprails and the Spur	8
Faces in the Street	10
The Wander-light	14
The Roaring Days	16
The Vagabond	19
Since Then	23
Sweeney	25
The Blue Mountains	28
Past Carin'	30
Sydney-side	32
Dan the Wreck	34
Ports of the Open Sea	37
To Jim	40
The Lights of Cobb and Co.	42
Middleton's Rouseabout	44

CONTENTS

	PAGE
One-Hundred-and-Three	46
Bertha	52
The Shearing-Shed	54
The Drover's Sweetheart	56
My Literary Friend	58
Ballad of the Rouseabout	59
Andy's Gone With Cattle	61
The Vanguard	62
Bill	63
When Your Pants Begin To Go	66
The Teams	68
When the World was Wide	70
Ballad of the Elder Son	74
The Southerly Buster	79
Out Back	81
Ballad of the Drover	84
After All	87
Black Bonnet	89
My Army, O My Army	93
Talbragar	95
Above Crow's Nest	97
The Shakedown on the Floor	99
Written Afterwards	101
The Green-hand Rouseabout	103
Scots of the Riverina	106
The Never-Never Land	108
After the War	111
The Jolly Dead March	116
For'ard	119

SELECTED POEMS OF HENRY LAWSON

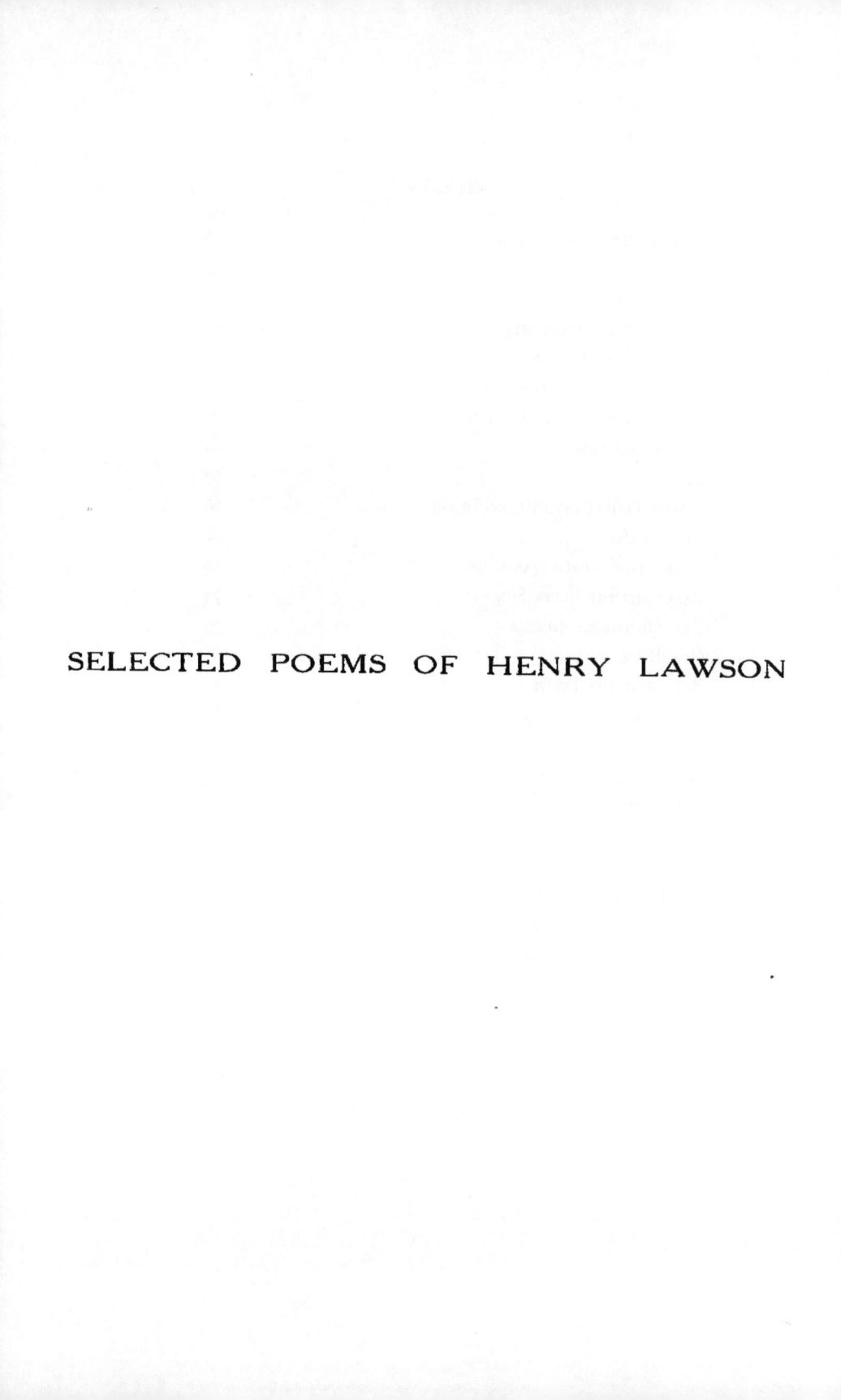

England Yet

SHE'S England yet! The nations never knew
    her;
Or, if they knew, were ready to forget.
She made new worlds that paid no homage to
    her,
    Because she called for none as for a debt.
The bullying power who deemed all nations craven,
    And that her star of destiny had set,
Was sure that she would seek a coward's haven—
    And tempted her, and found her England yet!

We learn our England, and we soon forget,
To learn again that she is England yet.

They watched Britannia ever looking forward,
    But could not see the things her children saw.
They watched in Southern seas her boats pull shoreward,
    But only marked the eyeglass, heard the "Haw!"
In tents, and bungalows, and outpost stations,
    Thin white men ruled for her, unseen, unheard,
Till millions of strange races and far nations
    Were ready to obey her at a word.

We learn our England, and in peace forget,
To learn in storm that she is England yet.

She's England yet; and men shall doubt no longer;
   And mourn no longer for what she has been.
She'll be a greater England and a stronger—
   A better England than the world has seen.
Our own, who reck not of a king's regalia,
   Tinsel of crowns, and courts that fume and fret,
Are fighting for her—fighting for Australia—
   And blasphemously hail her "England Yet!"

She's England yet, with little to regret—
Ay, more than ever, she'll be England yet!

1917

The Star of Australasia

WE boast no more of our bloodless flag that rose from a nation's slime;
    Better a shred of a deep-dyed rag from the storms of the olden time.
    From grander clouds in our "peaceful skies" than ever were there before
I tell you the Star of the South shall rise—in the lurid clouds of war.
It ever must be while blood is warm and the sons of men increase;
For ever the nations rose in storm, to rot in a deadly peace.
There'll come a point that we will not yield, no matter if right or wrong;
And man will fight on the battle-field while passion and pride are strong—
So long as he will not kiss the rod, and his stubborn spirit sours—
For the scorn of Nature and curse of God are heavy on peace like ours.

   .   .   .   .

There are boys out there by the western creeks, who hurry away from school
To climb the sides of the breezy peaks or dive in the shaded pool,
Who'll stick to their guns when the mountains quake to the tread of a mighty war,
And fight for Right or a Grand Mistake as men never fought before;

When the peaks are scarred and the sea-walls crack till the farthest hills vibrate,
And the world for a while goes rolling back in a storm of love and hate.

. . . .

There are boys to-day in the city slum and the home of wealth and pride
Who'll have one home when the storm is come, and fight for it side by side,
Who'll hold the cliffs against armoured hells that batter a coastal town,
Or grimly die in a hail of shells when the walls come crashing down.
And many a pink-white baby girl, the queen of her home to-day,
Will see the wings of the tempest whirl the mist of our dawn away—
Will live to shudder and stop her ears to the thud of the distant gun,
And know the sorrow that has no tears when a battle is lost and won—
As a mother or wife in the years to come will kneel, wild-eyed and white,
And pray to God in her darkened home for the "men in the fort to-night."

. . . .

But, oh! if the cavalry charge again as they did when the world was wide,
'Twill be grand in the ranks of a thousand men in that glorious race to ride,
And strike for all that is true and strong, for all that is grand and brave,
And all that ever shall be, so long as man has a soul to save.

But, oh! if the cavalry charge again as they did
  when the world was wide,
    'Twill be grand in the ranks of a thousand men
      in that glorious race to ride.
. . . .
And many a rickety son of a gun, on the tides
    of the future tossed,
  Will tell how battles were really won that History
    says were lost.

He must lift the saddle, and close his "wings," and shut his
    angels out,
And steel his heart for the end of things, who'd ride with a
    stockman scout,
When the race they ride on the battle track, and the waning
    distance hums,
When the shelled sky shrieks, and the rifles crack like stockwhips
    amongst the gums—
And the straight is reached and the field is gapped and the hoof-
    torn sward grows red
With the blood of those who are handicapped with iron and
    steel and lead;
And the gaps are filled, though unseen by eyes, with the spirit
    and with the shades
Of the world-wide rebel dead who'll rise and rush with the
    Bush Brigades.

    .   .   .   .

All creeds and trades will have soldiers there—give every class
    its due—
And there'll be many a clerk to spare for the pride of the
    jackeroo.
They'll fight for honour and fight for love, and a few will fight
    for gold,
For the devil below and for God above, as our fathers fought of
    old;
And some half-blind with exultant tears, and some stiff-lipped,
    stern-eyed,
For the pride of a thousand after-years and the old eternal
    pride;
The soul of the world they will feel and see in the chase and
    the grim retreat—
They'll know the glory of victory—and the grandeur of defeat.

The South will wake to a mighty change ere a hundred years are done
With arsenals west of the mountain range and every spur its gun.
And many a rickety son of a gun, on the tides of the future tossed,
Will tell how battles were really won that History says were lost,
Will trace the field with his pipe, and shirk the facts that are hard to explain,
As grey old mates of the diggings work the old ground over again—
How "This was our centre, and this a redoubt, and that was a scrub in the rear,
And this was the point where the Guards held out, and the enemy's lines were here."

. . . .

They'll tell the tales of the nights before and the tales of the ship and fort
Till the sons of Australia take to war as their fathers took to sport,
Till their breath comes deep and their eyes grow bright at the tales of our chivalry,
And every boy will want to fight, nor care what the cause may be—
When the children run to the doors and cry: "Oh, mother, the troops are come!"
And every heart in the town leaps high at the first loud thud of the drum.
They'll know, apart from its mystic charm, what music is at last,
When, proud as a boy with a broken arm, the regiment marches past.

And the veriest wreck in the drink-fiend's clutch, no matter how low or mean,
Will feel, when he hears that march, a touch of the man that he might have been.
And fools, when the fiends of war are out and the city skies aflame,
Will have something better to talk about than an absent woman's shame,
Will have something nobler to do by far than jest at a friend's expense,
Or blacken a name in a public bar or over a backyard fence.
And this we learn from the libelled past, though its methods were somewhat rude—
A Nation's born where the shells fall fast, or its lease of life renewed.
We in part atone for the ghoulish strife, and the crimes of the peace we boast,
And the better part of a people's life in the storm comes uppermost.

The self-same spirit that drives the man to the depths of drink and crime
Will do the deeds in the heroes' van that live till the end of time.
The living death in the lonely bush, the greed of the selfish town,
And even the creed of the outlawed push is chivalry—upside down.
'Twill be while ever our blood is hot, while ever the world goes wrong,
The nations rise in a war, to rot in a peace that lasts too long.
And southern Nation and southern State, aroused from their dream of ease,
Must sign in the Book of Eternal Fate their stormy histories.

1895

The Sliprails and the Spur

THE colours of the setting sun
    Withdrew across the Western land—
He raised the sliprails, one by one,
    And shot them home with trembling hand;
Her brown hands clung—her face grew pale—
    Ah! quivering chin and eyes that brim!—
One quick, fierce kiss across the rail,
    And, "Good-bye, Mary!" "Good-bye, Jim!"

Oh, he rides hard to race the pain
    Who rides from love, who rides from home;
But he rides slowly home again,
    Whose heart has learnt to love and roam.

A hand upon the horse's mane,
    And one foot in the stirrup set,
And, stooping back to kiss again,
    With "Good-bye, Mary! don't you fret!
When I come back"—he laughed for her—
    "We do not know how soon 'twill be;
I'll whistle as I round the spur—
    You let the sliprails down for me."

She gasped for sudden loss of hope,
    As, with a backward wave to her,
He cantered down the grassy slope
    And swiftly round the dark'ning spur.

THE SLIPRAILS AND THE SPUR

Black-pencilled panels standing high,
  And darkness fading into stars,
And, blurring fast against the sky,
  A faint white form beside the bars.

And often at the set of sun,
  In winter bleak and summer brown,
She'd steal across the little run,
  And shyly let the sliprails down.
And listen there when darkness shut
  The nearer spur in silence deep;
And when they called her from the hut
  Steal home and cry herself to sleep.

And he rides hard to dull the pain
  Who rides from one that loves him best . . . .
And he rides slowly back again,
  Whose restless heart must rove for rest.

1899

Faces in the Street

THEY lie, the men who tell us, for reasons of their own,
That want is here a stranger, and that misery's unknown;
For where the nearest suburb and the city proper meet
My window-sill is level with the faces in the street—
    Drifting past, drifting past,
    To the beat of weary feet—
While I sorrow for the owners of those faces in the street.

And cause I have to sorrow, in a land so young and fair,
To see upon those faces stamped the marks of Want and Care;
I look in vain for traces of the fresh and fair and sweet
In sallow, sunken faces that are drifting through the street—
    Drifting on, drifting on,
    To the scrape of restless feet;
I can sorrow for the owners of the faces in the street.

In hours before the dawning dims the starlight in the sky
The wan and weary faces first begin to trickle by,
Increasing as the moments hurry on with morning feet,
Till like a pallid river flow the faces in the street—
    Flowing in, flowing in,
    To the beat of hurried feet—
Ah! I sorrow for the owners of those faces in the street.

FACES IN THE STREET

The human river dwindles when 'tis past the hour of eight,
Its waves go flowing faster in the fear of being late;
But slowly drag the moments, whilst beneath the dust and heat
The city grinds the owners of the faces in the street—
    Grinding body, grinding soul,
    Yielding scarce enough to eat—
Oh! I sorrow for the owners of the faces in the street.

And then the only faces till the sun is sinking down
Are those of outside toilers and the idlers of the town,
Save here and there a face that seems a stranger in the street
Tells of the city's unemployed upon his weary beat—
    Drifting round, drifting round,
    To the tread of listless feet—
Ah! my heart aches for the owner of that sad face in the street.

And when the hours on lagging feet have slowly dragged away,
And sickly yellow gaslights rise to mock the going day,
Then, flowing past my window, like a tide in its retreat.
Again I see the pallid stream of faces in the street—
    Ebbing out, ebbing out,
    To the drag of tired feet,
While my heart is aching dumbly for the faces in the street.

And now all blurred and smirched with vice the day's sad end
    is seen,
For where the short "large hours" against the longer "small
    hours" lean,
With smiles that mock the wearer, and with words that half
    entreat,
Delilah pleads for custom at the corner of the street—
    Sinking down, sinking down,
    Battered wreck by tempests beat—
A dreadful, thankless trade is hers, that Woman of the Street.

But, ah! to dreader things than these our fair young city comes,
For in its heart are growing thick the filthy dens and slums,
Where human forms shall rot away in sties for swine unmeet,
And ghostly faces shall be seen unfit for any street—
  Rotting out, rotting out,
  For the lack of air and meat—
In dens of vice and horror that are hidden from the street.

I wonder would the apathy of wealthy men endure
Were all their windows level with the faces of the Poor?
Ah! Mammon's slaves, your knees shall knock, your hearts in terror beat,
When God demands a reason for the sorrows of the street,
  The wrong things and the bad things
  And the sad things that we meet
In the filthy lane and alley, and the cruel, heartless street.

I left the dreadful corner where the steps are never still,
And sought another window overlooking gorge and hill;
But when the night came dreary with the driving rain and sleet,
They haunted me—the shadows of those faces in the street,
  Flitting by, flitting by,
  Flitting by with noiseless feet,
And with cheeks that scarce were paler than the real ones in the street.

Once I cried: "O God Almighty! if Thy might doth still endure,
Now show me in a vision for the wrongs of Earth a cure."
And, lo, with shops all shuttered I beheld a city's street,
And in the warning distance heard the tramp of many feet,
  Coming near, coming near,
  To a drum's dull distant beat—
'Twas Despair's conscripted army that was marching down the street.

FACES IN THE STREET

Then, like a swollen river that has broken bank and wall,
The human flood came pouring with the red flags over all,
And kindled eyes all blazing bright with revolution's heat,
And flashing swords reflecting rigid faces in the street.
        Pouring on, pouring on,
        To a drum's loud threatening beat,
And the war-hymns and the cheering of the people in the street.

And so it must be while the world goes rolling round its course,
The warning pen shall write in vain, the warning voice grow
    hoarse,
But not until a city feels Red Revolution's feet
Shall its sad people miss awhile the terrors of the street—
        The dreadful, everlasting strife
        For scarcely clothes and meat
In that pent track of living death—the city's cruel street.

1888

The Wander-light

OH, my ways are strange ways and new ways and old ways,
And deep ways and steep ways and high ways and low;
I'm at home and at ease on a track that I know not,
And restless and lost on a road that I know.

    Then they heard the tent-poles clatter,
        And the fly in twain was torn—
    'Twas the soiled rag of a tatter
        Of the tent where I was born.
    Does it matter? Which is stranger—
        Brick or stone or calico?—
    There was One born in a manger
        Nineteen hundred years ago.

For my beds were camp beds and tramp beds and damp beds,
And my beds were dry beds on drought-stricken ground,
Hard beds and soft beds, and wide beds and narrow—
For my beds were strange beds the wide world round.

    And the old hag seemed to ponder
        With her grey head nodding slow—
    "He will dream, and he will wander
        Where but few would think to go.
    He will flee the haunts of tailors,
        He will cross the ocean wide,
    For his fathers they were sailors—
        All on his good father's side."

THE WANDER-LIGHT

I rest not, 'tis best not, the world is a wide one—
And, caged for a moment, I pace to and fro;
I see things and dree things and plan while I'm sleeping,
I wander for ever and dream as I go.

   And the old hag she was troubled
    As she bent above the bed,
  "He will dream things and he'll see things
    To come true when he is dead.
   He will see things all too plainly,
    And his fellows will deride,
   For his mothers they were gipsies—
    All on his good mother's side."

And my dreams are strange dreams, are day dreams, are grey dreams,
And my dreams are wild dreams, and old dreams and new;
They haunt me and daunt me with fears of the morrow—
My brothers they doubt me—but my dreams come true.

1903

The Roaring Days

THE night too quickly passes
   And we are growing old,
So let us fill our glasses
   And toast the Days of Gold;
When finds of wondrous treasure
   Set all the South ablaze,
And you and I were faithful mates
   All through the Roaring Days!

Then stately ships came sailing
   From every harbour's mouth,
And sought the Land of Promise
   That beaconed in the South;
Then southward streamed their streamers
   And swelled their canvas full
To speed the wildest dreamers
   E'er borne in vessel's hull.

Their shining Eldorado
   Beneath the southern skies
Was day and night for ever
   Before their eager eyes.
The brooding bush, awakened,
   Was stirred in wild unrest,
And all the year a human stream
   Went pouring to the West.

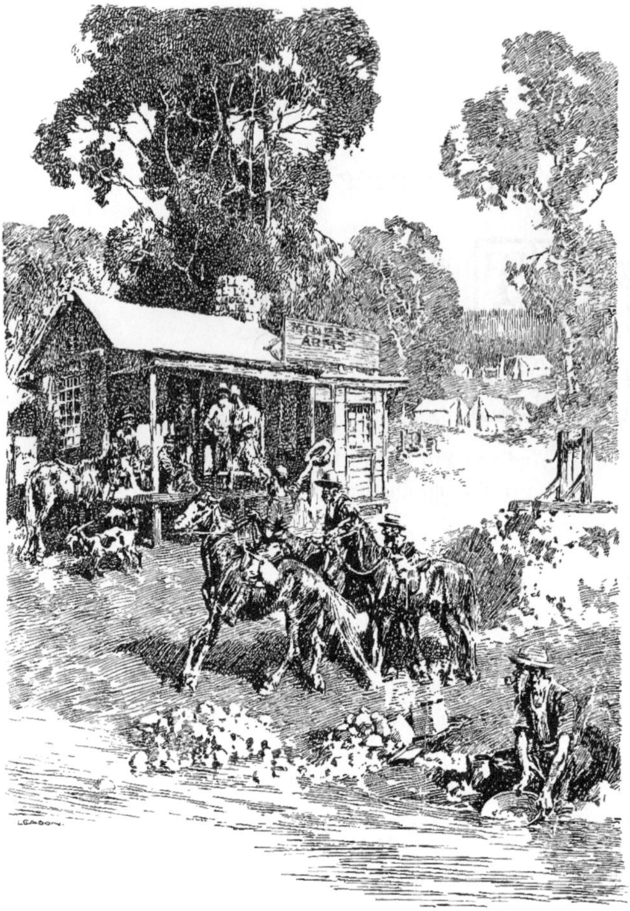
ARMS

THE ROARING DAYS

The rough bush roads re-echoed
   The bar-room's noisy din,
When troops of stalwart horsemen
   Dismounted at the inn.
And oft the hearty greetings
   And hearty clasp of hands
Would tell of sudden meetings
   Of friends from other lands.

And when the cheery camp-fire
   Explored the bush with gleams,
The camping-grounds were crowded
   With caravans of teams;
Then home the jests were driven,
   And good old songs were sung,
And choruses were given
   The strength of heart and lung.

Oft when the camps were dreaming,
   And fires began to pale,
Through rugged ranges gleaming
   Swept on the Royal Mail.
Behind six foaming horses,
   And lit by flashing lamps,
Old Cobb and Co., in royal state,
   Went dashing past the camps.

Oh, who would paint a goldfield,
   And paint the picture right,
As old Adventure saw it
   In early morning's light?
The yellow mounds of mullock
   With spots of red and white,
The scattered quartz that glistened
   Like diamonds in light;

THE ROARING DAYS

The azure line of ridges,
  The bush of darkest green,
The little homes of calico
  That dotted all the scene.
The flat straw hats, with ribands,
  That old engravings show—
The dress that still reminds us
  Of sailors, long ago.

I hear the fall of timber
  From distant flats and fells,
The pealing of the anvils
  As clear as little bells,
The rattle of the cradle,
  The clack of windlass-boles,
The flutter of the crimson flags
  Above the golden holes.

Ah, then their hearts were bolder,
  And if Dame Fortune frowned
Their swags they'd lightly shoulder
  And tramp to other ground.
Oh, they were lion-hearted
  Who gave our country birth!
Stout sons, of stoutest fathers born,
  From all the lands on earth!

Those golden days are vanished,
  And altered is the scene:
The diggings are deserted,
  The camping-grounds are green;
The flaunting flag of progress
  Is in the West unfurled,
The mighty Bush with iron rails
  Is tethered to the world.

1889

The Vagabond

WHITE handkerchiefs wave from the short
    black pier
    As we glide to the grand old sea—
    But the song of my heart is for none to hear
    If none of them waves for me.
    A roving, roaming life is mine,
  Ever by field or flood—
For not far back in my father's line
  Was a dash of the Gipsy blood.

Flax and tussock and fern,
  Gum and mulga and sand,
Reef and palm—but my fancies turn
  Ever away from land;
Strange wild cities in ancient state,
  Range and river and tree,
Snow and ice. But my star of fate
  Is ever across the sea.

A god-like ride on a thundering sea,
  When all but the stars are blind—
A desperate race from Eternity
  With a gale-and-a-half behind.
A jovial spree in the cabin at night,
  A song on the rolling deck,
A lark ashore with the ships in sight,
  Till—a wreck goes down with a wreck.

THE VAGABOND

A smoke and a yarn on the deck by day,
  When life is a waking dream,
And care and trouble so far away
  That out of your life they seem.
A roving spirit in sympathy,
  Who has travelled the whole world o'er—
My heart forgets, in a week at sea,
  The trouble of years on shore.

A rolling stone!—'tis a saw for slaves—
  Philosophy false as old—
Wear out or break 'neath the feet of knaves,
  Or rot in your bed of mould!
But I'd rather trust to the darkest skies
  And the wildest seas that roar,
Or die, where the stars of Nations rise,
  In the stormy clouds of war.

Cleave to your country, home, and friends,
  Die in a sordid strife—
You can count your friends on your finger ends
  In the critical hours of life.
Sacrifice all for the family's sake,
  Bow to their selfish rule!
Slave till your big soft heart they break—
  The heart of the "family fool."

I've never a love that can sting my pride,
  Nor a friend to prove untrue;
For I leave my love ere the turning tide,
  And my friends are all too new.
The curse of the Powers on a peace like ours,
  With its greed and its treachery—
A stranger's hand, and a stranger-land,
  And the rest of the world for me!

But why be bitter? The world is cold
   To one with a frozen heart;
New friends are often so like the old,
   They seem of the Past a part—
As a better part of the past appears,
   When enemies, parted long,
Are come together in kinder years,
   With their better nature strong.

I had a friend, ere my first ship sailed,
   A friend that I never deserved—
For the selfish strain in my blood prevailed
   As soon as my turn was served.
And the memory haunts my heart with shame—
   Or, rather, the pride that's there;
In different guises, but soul the same.
   I meet him everywhere.

I had a chum. When the times were tight
   We starved in Australian scrubs;
We froze together in parks at night,
   And laughed together in pubs.
And I often hear a laugh like his
   From a sense of humour keen,
And catch a glimpse in a passing phiz
   Of his broad, good-humoured grin.

And I had a love—'twas a love to prize—
   But I never went back again . . .
I have seen the light of her kind grey eyes
   In many a face since then.

THE VAGABOND

The sailors say 'twill be rough to-night,
    As they fasten the hatches down;
The south is black, and the bar is white,
    And the drifting smoke is brown.
The gold has gone from the western haze,
    The sea-birds circle and swarm—
But we shall have plenty of sunny days,
    And little enough of storm.

The hill is hiding the short black pier,
    As the last white signal's seen;
The points run in, and the houses veer,
    And the great bluff stands between.
So darkness swallows each far white speck
    On many a wharf and quay;
The night comes down on a restless deck,—
    Grim cliffs—and—The Open Sea!

1895

Since Then

I MET Jack Ellis in town to-day—
    Jack Ellis—my old mate, Jack.
Ten years ago, from the Castlereagh,
We carried our swags together away
    To the Never-Again, Out Back.

But times have altered since those old days,
    And the times have changed the men.
Ah, well! there's little to blame or praise—
Jack Ellis and I have tramped long ways
    On different tracks since then.

His hat was battered, his coat was green,
    The toes of his boots were through,
But the pride was his! It was I felt mean—
I wished that my collar was not so clean,
    Nor the clothes I wore so new.

He saw me first, and he knew 'twas I—
    The holiday swell he met.
Why have we no faith in each other? Ah, why?—
He made as though he would pass me by,
    For he thought that I might forget.

He ought to have known me better than that,
    By the tracks we tramped far out—
The sweltering scrub and the blazing flat,
When the heat came down through each old felt hat
    In the hell-born western drought.

    .   .   .   .   .   .

SINCE THEN

He took my hand in a distant way
    (I thought how we parted last),
And we seemed like men who have nought to say
And who meet—"Good-day," and who part—
    "Good-day,"
Who never have shared the past.

I asked him in for a drink with me—
    Jack Ellis—my old mate, Jack—
But his manner no longer was careless and free,
He followed, but not with the grin that he
    Wore always in days Out Back.

I tried to live in the past once more—
    Or the present and past combine,
But the days between I could not ignore—
I couldn't but notice the clothes he wore,
    And he couldn't but notice mine.

He placed his glass on the polished bar,
    And he wouldn't fill up again;
For he is prouder than most men are—
Jack Ellis and I have tramped too far
    On different tracks since then.

He said that he had a mate to meet,
    And "I'll see you again," said he,
Then he hurried away through the crowded street,
And the rattle of buses and scrape of feet
    Seemed suddenly loud to me.

1895

Sweeney

IT was somewhere in September, and the sun was
    going down,
When I came, in search of copy, to a Darling-River
    town;
"Come-and-Have-a-Drink" we'll call it—'tis a fitting
    name, I think—
And 'twas raining, for a wonder, up at Come-and-Have-a-Drink.

Underneath the pub verandah I was resting on a bunk
When a stranger rose before me, and he said that he was drunk;
He apologized for speaking; there was no offence, he swore;
But he somehow seemed to fancy that he'd seen my face before.

"No erfence," he said. I told him that he needn't mention it,
For I might have met him somewhere; I had travelled round a
    bit,
And I knew a lot of fellows in the Bush and in the streets—
But a fellow can't remember all the fellows that he meets.

Very old and thin and dirty were the garments that he wore,
Just a shirt and pair of trousers, and a boot, and nothing more;
He was wringing-wet, and really in a sad and sinful plight,
And his hat was in his left hand, and a bottle in his right.

He agreed: You can't remember all the chaps you chance to meet,
And he said his name was Sweeney—people lived in Sussex-
    street.
He was camping in a stable, but he swore that he was right,
"Only for the blanky horses walkin' over him all night."

He'd apparently been fighting, for his face was black-and-blue,
And he looked as though the horses had been treading on him,
   too;
But an honest, genial twinkle in the eye that wasn't hurt
Seemed to hint of something better, spite of drink and rags
   and dirt.

It appeared that he mistook me for a long-lost mate of his—
One of whom I was the image, both in figure and in phiz—
(He'd have had a letter from him if the chap was livin' still,
For they'd carried swags together from the Gulf to Broken Hill).

Sweeney yarned awhile and hinted that his folks were doing well,
And he told me that his father kept the Southern Cross Hotel;
And I wondered if his absence was regarded as a loss
When he left the elder Sweeney—landlord of the Southern
   Cross.

He was born in Parramatta, and he said, with humour grim,
That he'd like to see the city ere the liquor finished him,
But he couldn't raise the money. He was damned if he could
   think
What the Government was doing. Here he offered me a drink.

I declined—*'twas* self-denial—and I lectured him on booze,
Using all the hackneyed arguments that preachers mostly use;
Things I'd heard in temperance lectures (I was young and rather
   green),
And I ended by referring to the man he might have been.

Then a wise expression struggled with the bruises on his face,
Though his argument had scarcely any bearing on the case:

"What's the good o' keepin' sober? Fellers rise and fellers fall;
What I might have been and wasn't doesn't trouble me at all."

But he couldn't stay to argue, for his beer was nearly gone.
He was glad, he said, to meet me, and he'd see me later on,
But he guessed he'd have to go and get his bottle filled again;
And he gave a lurch and vanished in the darkness and the rain.

. . . : . . . .

And of afternoons in cities, when the rain is on the land,
Visions come to me of Sweeney with his bottle in his hand,
With the stormy night behind him, and the pub verandah-post—
And I wonder why he haunts me more than any other ghost.

I suppose he's tramping somewhere where the bushmen carry swags,
Dragging round the western stations with his empty tucker-bags;
And I fancy that, of evenings, when the track is growing dim,
What he "might have been and wasn't" comes along and troubles him.

1893

The Blue Mountains

ABOVE the ashes straight and tall,
   Through ferns with moisture dripping,
I climb beneath the sandstone wall,
   My feet on mosses slipping.

Like ramparts round the valley's edge
   The tinted cliffs are standing,
With many a broken wall and ledge,
   And many a rocky landing.

And round about their rugged feet
   Deep ferny dells are hidden
In shadowed depths, whence dust and heat
   Are banished and forbidden.

The stream that, crooning to itself,
   Comes down a tireless rover,
Flows calmly to the rocky shelf,
   And there leaps bravely over.

Now pouring down, now lost in spray
   When mountain breezes sally,
The water strikes the rock midway,
   And leaps into the valley.

    .   .   .   .   .

THE BLUE MOUNTAINS

Now in the west the colours change,
    The blue with crimson blending;
Behind the far Dividing Range
    The sun is fast descending.

And mellowed day comes o'er the place,
    And softens ragged edges:
The rising moon's great placid face
    Looks gravely o'er the ledges.

1888

Past Carin'

NOW up and down the sidling brown
    The great black crows are flyin',
And down below the spur, I know,
    Another "milker's" dyin';
The crops have withered from the ground,
    The tank's clay bed is glarin',
But from my heart no tear nor sound,
    For I have got past carin'—
        Past worryin' or carin'—
        Past feelin' aught or carin';
        But from my heart no tear nor sound,
        For I have got past carin'.

Through Death and Trouble, turn about,
    Through hopeless desolation,
Through flood and fever, fire and drought,
    And slavery and starvation;
Through childbirth, sickness, hurt, and blight,
    And nervousness an' scarin',
Through bein' left alone at night,
    I've come to be past carin'.
        Past botherin' or carin',
        Past feelin' and past carin';
        Through city cheats and neighbours' spite,
        I've come to be past carin'.

Our first child took, in days like these,
    A cruel week in dyin',
All day upon her father's knees,
    Or on my poor breast lyin':

Now up and down the sidling brown
  The great black crows are flyin',
And down below the spur, I know,
  Another "milker's" dyin';
The crops have withered from the ground,
  The tank's clay bed is glarin',
But from my heart no tear nor sound,
  For I have got past carin'—

PAST CARIN'

The tears we shed—the prayers we said
  Were awful, wild—despairin'!
I've pulled three through and buried two
  Since then—and I'm past carin'.
      I've grown to be past carin',
      Past lookin' up or carin';
      I've pulled three through and buried two
      Since then, and I'm past carin'.

'Twas ten years first, then came the worst,
  All for a barren clearin',
I thought, I thought my heart would burst
  When first my man went shearin';
He's drovin' in the great North-west,
  I don't know how he's farin';
And I, the one that loved him best,
  Have grown to be past carin'.
      I've grown to be past carin',
      Past waitin' and past wearin':
      The girl that waited long ago,
      Has lived to be past carin'.

My eyes are dry, I cannot cry,
  I've got no heart for breakin',
But where it was, in days gone by,
  A dull and empty achin'.
My last boy ran away from me—
  I know my temper's wearin'—
But now I only wish to be
  Beyond all signs of carin'.
      Past wearyin' or carin',
      Past feelin' and despairin';
      And now I only wish to be
      Beyond all signs of carin'.

1899

Sydney-side

WHERE'S the steward?—Bar-room steward! Berth?
    Oh, any berth will do—
I have left a three-pound billet just to come along
    with you.
Brighter shines the Star of Rovers on a world that's
    growing wide,
But I think I'd give a kingdom for a glimpse of Sydney-side.

Run of rocky shelves at sunrise, with their base on ocean's bed;
Homes of Coogee, homes of Bondi, and the lighthouse on South
    Head;
For in loneliness and hardship—and with just a touch of pride—
Has my heart been taught to whisper, "You belong to Sydney-
    side."

Oh, there never dawned a morning, in the long and lonely days,
But I thought I saw the ferries streaming out across the bays—
And as fresh and fair in fancy did the picture rise again
As the sunrise flushed the city from Woollahra to Balmain;

With the sunny water frothing round the liners black and red,
And the coastal schooners working by the loom of Bradley's
    Head,
With the whistles and the sirens that re-echo far and wide—
All the life and light and beauty that belong to Sydney-side.

And the dreary cloud-line never veiled the end of one day more,
But the City set in jewels rose before me from "The Shore."
Round the sea-world shine the beacons of a thousand ports o' call,
But the harbour-lights of Sydney are the grandest of them all.

Toiling out beyond Coolgardie—heart and back and spirit broke,
Where the Rover's star gleams redly in the desert by the soak—
"But," says one mate to the other, "brace your lip and do not fret,
We will laugh on trams and buses—Sydney's in the same place yet."

Working in the South in winter, to the waist in dripping fern,
Where the local spirit hungers for each "saxpence" that you earn—
We can stand it for a season, for our world is growing wide,
And they all are friends and strangers who belong to Sydney-side.

"T'other-siders! T'other-siders!" Yet we wake the dusty dead,
For 'twas we that sent the backward province fifty years ahead:
We it is that trim Australia—making narrow country wide—
Yet we're always T'other-siders till we sail for Sydney-side.

1898

Dan the Wreck

TALL, and stout, and solid-looking,
    Yet a wreck;
None would think Death's finger's hooking
    Him from deck.
Cause of half the fun that's started—
    Hard-case Dan—
Isn't like a broken-hearted,
    Ruined man.

Walking-coat from tail to throat is
    Frayed and greened—
Like a man whose other coat is
    Being cleaned;
Gone for ever round the edging
    Past repair—
Waistcoat pockets frayed with dredging
    After "sprats" no longer there.

Wearing summer boots in June, or
    Slippers worn and old—
Like a man whose other shoon are
    Getting soled.
Pants? They're far from being recent—
    But, perhaps, I'd better not—
Says they are the only decent
    Pair he's got.

And his hat, I am afraid, is
   Troubling him—
Past all lifting to the ladies
   By the brim.
But, although he'd hardly strike a
   Girl, would Dan,
Yet he wears his wreckage like a
   Gentleman.

Once—no matter how the rest dressed—
   Up or down—
Once, they say, he was the best-dressed
   Man in town.
Must have been before I knew him—
   Now you'd scarcely care to meet
And be noticed talking to him
   In the street.

Drink the cause, and dissipation,
   That is clear—
Maybe friend or kind relation
   Cause of beer.
And the talking fool, who never
   Reads or thinks,
Says, from hearsay: "Yes, he's clever;
   But, you know, he drinks."

Where he lives, or how, or wherefore,
   No one knows;
Lost his real friends, and therefore
   Lost his foes.
Had, no doubt, his own romances—
   Met his fate;
Tortured, doubtless, by the chances
   And the luck that comes too late.

Now and then his boots are polished,
  Collar clean,
And the worst grease stains abolished
  With ammonia or benzine:
Hints of some attempt to shove him
  From the taps,
Or of someone left to love him—
  Sister, p'r'aps.

After all, he is a grafter,
  Earns his cheer—
Keeps the room in roars of laughter
  When he gets outside a beer.
Yarns that would fall flat from others
  He can tell;
How he spent his stuff, my brothers,
  You know well.

Manner puts a man in mind of
  Old club balls and evening dress,
Ugly with a handsome kind of
  Ugliness.
One of those we'd say of, grimly,
  At the morgue—or mean hotel
Where they hold the inquests dimly:
  "He looked well!"

  .   .   .   .   .

I may be, so goes the rumour,
  Bad as Dan;
But I have not got the humour
  Of the man:
Nor the sight—well, deem it blindness,
  As the general public do—
And the love of human kindness,
  Or the grit to see it through.

1896

Ports of the Open Sea

DOWN here, where the ships loom large in
    The gloom when the sea-storms veer,
Down here on the south-west margin
    Of the western hemisphere,
Where the might of a world-wide ocean
    Round the youngest land rolls free—
Storm-bound from the World's commotion
    Lie the Ports of the Open Sea.

By the bluff where the grey sand reaches
    To the kerb of the spray-swept street,
By the sweep of the black sand beaches
    From the main-road travellers' feet,
By the heights, like a work Titanic,
    Begun ere the gods' work ceased,
By a bluff-lined coast volcanic
    Lie the Ports of the wild South-east.

By the steeps of the snow-capped ranges,
    By the scarped and terraced hills—
Far away from the swift life-changes,
    From the wear of the strife that kills—
Where the land in the spring seems younger
    Than a land of the Earth might be—
Oh! the hearts of the rovers hunger
    For the Ports of the Open Sea.

But the captains watch and harken
    For a sign of the South Sea's wrath—
Let the face of the South-east darken,
    And they turn to the ocean path.
Ay, the sea-boats dare not linger,
    Whatever the cargo be,
When the South-east lifts a finger
    By the Ports of the Open Sea.

Down South by the bleak Bluff faring,
    Or North where the Three Kings wait,
The storms of the South-east daring,
    They race through the foam-tossed strait.
Astern, where a white-winged roamer
    Found death in the tempest's roar,
The wash of the foam-flaked comber
    Runs green to the black-ribbed shore.

For the South-east lands are dread lands
    To the sailor high in the shrouds,
Where the low clouds loom like headlands,
    And the black bluffs blur like clouds.
When the breakers rage to windward
    And the lights are masked a-lee,
And the sunken rocks run inward
    To a Port of the Open Sea.

But oh! for the South-east weather—
    The sweep of the three-days' gale—
When far through the flax and heather
    The spindrift drives like hail.
Glory to man's creations
    That drive where the gale grows gruff,
When the homes of the sea-coast stations
    Flash white from the dark'ning bluff!

PORTS OF THE OPEN SEA

When the swell of the South-east rouses
   The wrath of the Maori sprite,
And the brown folk flee their houses
   To crouch in the flax by night,
And wait as they long have waited—
   In fear as the brown folk be—
The wave of destruction fated
   For the Ports of the Open Sea.

     .   .   .   .

Grey cloud to the mountain bases,
   Wild boughs in their rush and sweep,
The rounded hills in their places
   With tussocks like flying sheep;
The storm-bird alone and soaring
   O'er grasses and fern and tree;
And the beaches of boulder roaring
   The Hymn of the Open Sea.

1897

To Jim

I GAZE upon my son once more
    With eyes and heart that tire,
  As solemnly he stands before
    The screen drawn round the fire;
  With hands behind clasped hand in hand,
    Now loosely and now fast—
Just as his fathers used to stand
  For generations past.

A fair and slight and childish form,
  With big brown thoughtful eyes—
God help him, for a life of storm
  And stress before him lies.
A wanderer and a gipsy wild,
  I learnt the world and know,
For I was such another child—
  Ah, many years ago!

But in those dreamy eyes of him
  There is no hint of doubt—
I wish that you could tell me, Jim,
  The things you dream about.
You are a child of field and flood,
  For with the Gipsy strain
A strong Norwegian sailor's blood
  Runs red through every vein.

TO JIM

Dream on, my son, that all is true
   And things not what they seem—
'Twill be a bitter day when you
   Are wakened from your dream.
Be true, and slander never stings,
   Be straight, and all may frown—
You'll have the strength to grapple things
   That dragged your father down.

These lines I write with bitter tears
   And failing heart and hand,
But you will read in after years,
   And you will understand;
You'll hear the slander of the crowd,
   They'll whisper tales of shame:
But days will come when you'll be proud
   To bear your father's name.

1905

The Lights of Cobb and Co.

FIRE lighted; on the table a meal for sleepy men;
A lantern in the stable; a jingle now and then;
The mail-coach looming darkly by light of moon and
 star;
The growl of sleepy voices; a candle in the bar;
A stumble in the passage of folk with wits abroad;
A swear-word from a bedroom—the shout of "All aboard!"
"Tchk tchk! Git-up!" "Hold fast, there!" and down the range
 we go;
Five hundred miles of scattered camps will watch for Cobb
 and Co.

Old coaching towns already decaying for their sins;
Uncounted "Half-Way Houses," and scores of "Ten-Mile Inns;"
The riders from the stations by lonely granite peaks;
The black-boy for the shepherds on sheep and cattle creeks;
The roaring camps of Gulgong, and many a "Digger's Rest";
The diggers on the Lachlan; the huts of Farthest West;
Some twenty thousand exiles who sailed for weal or woe—
The bravest hearts of twenty lands will wait for Cobb and Co.

The morning star has vanished, the frost and fog are gone,
In one of those grand mornings which but on mountains dawn;
A flask of friendly whisky—each other's hopes we share—
And throw our top-coats open to drink the mountain air.
The roads are rare to travel, and life seems all complete;
The grind of wheels on gravel, the trot of horses' feet,
The trot, trot, trot and canter, as down the spur we go—
The green sweeps to horizons blue that call for Cobb and Co.

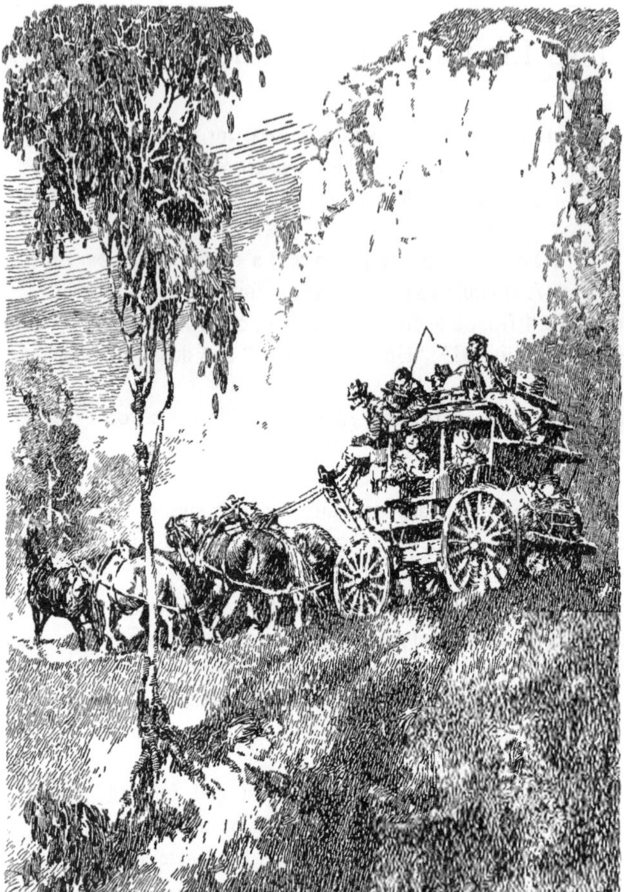

THE LIGHTS OF COBB AND CO.

We take a bright girl actress through western dusts and damps,
To bear the home-world message, and sing for sinful camps,
To stir our hearts and break them, wild hearts that hope and ache—
(Ah! when she thinks again of these her own must nearly break!)
Five miles this side the gold-field, a loud, triumphant shout:
Five hundred cheering diggers have snatched the horses out:
With "Auld Lang Syne" in chorus, through roaring camps they go
That cheer for her, and cheer for Home, and cheer for Cobb and Co.

Three lamps above the ridges and gorges dark and deep,
A flash on sandstone cuttings where sheer the sidlings sweep,
A flash on shrouded waggons, on water ghastly white;
Weird bush and scattered remnants of "rushes in the night;"
Across the swollen river a flash beyond the ford:
Ride hard to warn the driver! He's drunk or mad, good Lord!
But on the bank to westward a broad and cheerful glow—
New camps extend across the plains new routes for Cobb and Co.

Swift scramble up the sidling where teams climb inch by inch;
Pause, bird-like, on the summit—then breakneck down the pinch;
By clear, ridge-country rivers, and gaps where tracks run high,
Where waits the lonely horseman, cut clear against the sky;
Past haunted half-way houses—where convicts made the bricks—
Scrub-yards and new bark shanties, we dash with five and six;
Through stringy-bark and blue-gum, and box and pine we go—
A hundred miles shall see to-night the lights of Cobb and Co!

1897

Middleton's Rouseabout

TALL and freckled and sandy,
    Face of a country lout;
  This was the picture of Andy,
    Middleton's Rouseabout.

Type of a coming nation
    In the land of cattle and sheep;
Worked on Middleton's station,
    Pound a week and his keep;

On Middleton's wide dominions
    Plied the stockwhip and shears;
Hadn't any opinions,
    Hadn't any "idears."

Swiftly the years went over,
    Liquor and drought prevailed;
Middleton went as a drover
    After his station had failed.

Type of a careless nation,
    Men who are soon played out,
Middleton was:—and his station
    Was bought by the Rouseabout.

MIDDLETON'S ROUSEABOUT

    Flourishing beard and sandy,
      Tall and solid and stout;
    This is the picture of Andy,
      Middleton's Rouseabout.

    Now on his own dominions
      Works with his overseers;
    Hasn't any opinions,
      Hasn't any idears.

1890

One-Hundred-and-Three

WITH the frame of a man and the face of a boy, and
   a manner strangely wild,
And the great, wide, wondering, innocent eyes of a
   silent-suffering child;
With his hideous dress and his heavy boots, he drags
   to Eternity—
And the Warder says, in a softened tone: "Catch step, One-
   Hundred-and-Three."

'Tis a ghastly parody of drill—or a travesty of work—
But One-Hundred-and-Three he catches step with a start, a
   shuffle and jerk.
He is silenced and starved and "drilled" in gaol—and a waster's
   son was he:
His sins were written before he was born (Keep step! One-
   Hundred-and-Three.)

They shut a man in the four-by-eight, with a six-inch slit for air.
Twenty-three hours of the twenty-four, to brood on his virtues
   there.
The dead stone walls and the iron door close in like iron bands
On eyes that had followed the distant haze out there on the
   Level Lands.

Bread and water and hominy, and a scrag of meat and a spud.
A Bible and thin flat Book of Rules, to cool a strong man's
   blood;
They take the spoon from the cell at night—and a stranger would
   think it odd:
But a man might sharpen it on the floor, and go to his own
   Great God.

ONE-HUNDRED-AND-THREE

One-Hundred-and-Three, it is hard to believe that you saddled your horse at dawn,
And strolled through the bush with a girl at eve, or lolled with her on the lawn.
There were picnic parties in sunny bays, and ships on the shining sea;
There were foreign ports in the glorious days—(Hold up, One-Hundred-and-Three!)

A man came out at exercise time from one of the cells to-day:
'Twas the ghastly spectre of one I knew, and I thought he was far away;
We dared not speak, but he signed "Farewell—fare—well," and I knew by this
And the number stamped on his clothes (not sewn) that a heavy sentence was his.

Where five men do the work of a boy, with warders *not* to see—
It is sad and bad and uselessly mad, it is ugly as it can be,
From the flower-beds shaped to fit the gaol, in circle and line absurd,
To the gilded weathercock on the church, agape like a strangled bird—

Agape like a strangled bird in the sun, and I wonder what he can see—
The Fleet come in, and the Fleet go out? (Hold up, One-Hundred-and-Three!)
The glorious sea, and the bays and Bush, and the distant mountains blue—
(Keep step, keep step, One-Hundred-and-Three, for my heart is halting too).

The great, round church with its volume of sound, where we dare
   not turn our eyes—
They take us there from our separate hells to sing of Paradise;
The High Church service swells and swells where the tinted
   Christs look down—
It is easy to see who is weary and faint and weareth the thorny
   crown.

Though every creed hath its Certain Hope, yet here, in hopeless
   doubt,
Despairing prisoners faint in church, and the warders carry
   them out.
There are swift-made signs that are not to God as they march
   us hellward then;
It is hard to believe that we knelt as boys to "For ever and ever,
   Amen."

Rules, regulations—Red Tape and rules; all and alike they bind:
Under separate treatment place the deaf; in the dark cell shut
   the blind!
And somewhere down in his sandstone tomb, with never a word
   to save,
One-Hundred-and-Three is keeping step, as he'll keep it to his
   grave.

The press is printing its smug, smug lies, and paying its shameful
   debt—
It speaks of the comforts that prisoners have, and "holidays"
   prisoners get.
The visitors come with their smug, smug smiles through the
   gaol on a working day,
And the public hears with its large, large ears what authorities
   have to say.

They lay their fingers on well-hosed walls, and they tread on
    the polished floor;
They peep in the generous, shining cans with their ration Number
    Four.
And the visitors go with their smug, smug smiles; the reporters'
    work is done;
*Stand up! my men, who have done your time on Ration Number
    One!*

He shall be buried alive without meat, for a day and a night
    unheard,
If he speak a word to his fellow-corpse—who died for want of
    a word.
He shall be punished, and he shall be starved, and he shall in
    darkness rot.
He shall be murdered body and soul—and God saith: "Thou
    shalt not."

I've seen the remand-yard men go forth by the subway out of
    the yard—
And I've seen them come in with a foolish grin and a sentence
    of Three Years Hard.
They send a half-starved man to the Court, where the hearts of
    men they carve—
Then feed him up in the hospital to give him the strength to
    starve.

You get the gaol-dust into your throat, your skin goes the dead
    gaol-white;
You get the gaol-whine in your voice and in every letter you
    write.
And into your eyes comes the bright gaol-light—not the glare of
    the world's distraught,
Not the hunted look, nor the guilty look, but the awful look of
    the Caught.

The brute is a brute, and a kind man kind, and the strong heart
 does not fail—
A crawler's a crawler everywhere, but a man is a man in gaol;
For the kindness of man to man is great when penned in a
 sandstone pen—
The public call us the "criminal class," but the warders call us
 "the men."

We crave for sunlight, we crave for meat, we crave for the
 Might-have-Been,
But the cruellest thing in the walls of a gaol is the craving for
 nicotine.
Yet the spirit of Christ is in every place where the soul of a
 man can dwell—
It comes like tobacco in prison, or like news to the separate cell.

The champagne lady comes home from the course in charge of
 the criminal swell—
They carry her in from the motor-car to the lift in the Grand
 Hotel;
But armed with the savage Habituals Act they are waiting for
 you and me—
And drunkards in judgment on drunkards sit, (Keep step, One-
 Hundred-and-Three!)

The clever scoundrels are all outside, and the moneyless mugs in
 gaol—
Men do twelve months for a mad wife's lies or Life for a
 strumpet's tale.
If the people knew what the warders know, and felt as the
 prisoners feel—
If the people knew, they would storm their gaols as they stormed
 the old Bastille.

Warders and prisoners, all alike, in a dead rot, dry and slow—
The author must not write for his own, and the tailor must not sew.
The billet-bound officers dare not speak, and discharged men dare not tell,
Though many and many an innocent man must brood in this barren hell.

Ay! clang the spoon on the iron floor, and shove in the bread with your toe,
And shut with a bang the iron door, and clank the bolt—just so;
But One-Hundred-and-Three is near the End when the clonking gaol-bell sounds—
He cannot swallow the milk they send when the doctor has gone his rounds.

. . . .

They have smuggled him out to the hospital, with no one to tell the tale,
But it's little that doctor or nurses can do for the patient from Starvinghurst Gaol.
The blanket and screen are ready to draw. . . . There are footsteps light and free—
And the angels are whispering over his bed: "Keep step—One-Hundred-and-Three."

1908

Bertha

IDE, solemn eyes that question me,
    Wee hand that pats my head—
  Where only two have stroked before,
    And both of them are dead.
  "Ah, poo-ah Daddy mine," she says,
    With wondrous sympathy—
Oh, baby girl, you don't know how
    You break the heart in me!

Let friends and kinsfolk work their worst,
    Let all say what they will,
Your baby arms go around my neck—
    I'm your own Daddy still!
And you kiss me and I kiss you,
    Fresh kisses, frank and free—
Ah, baby girl, you don't know how
    You break the heart in me!

When I was good I dreamed that when
    The snow showed in my hair
A household angel in her teens
    Would flit about my chair,
To comfort me as I grew old;
    But that shall never be—
Ah, baby girl, you don't know how
    You break the heart in me!

BERTHA

But one shall love me while I live,
    And soothe my troubled head,
And never brook an unkind word
    Of me when I am dead.
Her eyes shall light to hear my name
    Howe'er disgraced it be—
Ah, baby girl, you don't know how
    You help the heart in me!

1903

The Shearing-Shed

"THE ladies are coming," the super says
    To the shearers sweltering there,
And "the ladies" means in the shearing-shed:
    "Don't cut 'em too bad. Don't swear."
The ghost of a pause in the shed's rough heart,
    And lower is bowed each head;
And nothing is heard save a whispered word
    And the roar of the shearing-shed.

The tall, shy rouser has lost his wits,
    And his limbs are all astray;
He leaves a fleece on the shearing-board,
    And his broom in the shearer's way.
There's a curse in store for that jackeroo
    As down by the wall he slants—
And the ringer bends with his legs askew
    And wishes he'd "patched them pants."

They are girls from the city. (Our hearts rebel
    As we squint at their dainty feet.)
And they gush and say in a girly way
    That "the dear little lambs" are "sweet."
And Bill the Ringer, who'd scorn the use
    Of a childish word like damn,
Would give a pound that his tongue were loose
    As he tackles a lively lamb.

THE SHEARING-SHED

Swift thoughts of homes in the coastal towns—
   Or rivers and waving grass—
And a weight on our hearts that we cannot define
   That comes as the ladies pass;
But the rouser ventures a nervous dig
   With his thumb in the next man's back;
And Bogan says to his pen-mate: "Twig
   The style of the last un, Jack."

Jack Moonlight gives her a careless glance—
   Then catches his breath with pain;
His strong hand shakes, and the sunlights dance
   As he bends to his work again.
But he's well disguised in a bristling beard,
   Bronzed skin, and his shearer's dress;
And whatever he knew or hoped or feared
   Was hard for his mates to guess.

Jack Moonlight, wiping his broad, white brow,
   Explains, with a doleful smile:
"A stitch in the side," and "I'm all right now"—
   But he leans on the beam awhile,
And gazes out in the blazing noon
   On the clearing, brown and bare . .
She had come and gone—like a breath of June
   In December's heat and glare.

1897

The Drover's Sweetheart

AN hour before the sun goes down
    Behind the ragged boughs,
I go across the little run
    And bring the dusty cows;
And once I used to sit and rest
    Beneath the fading dome,
For there was one that I loved best
    Who'd bring the cattle home.

Our yard is fixed with double bails;
    Round one the grass is green,
The Bush is growing through the rails,
    The spike is rusted in;
It was from there his freckled face
    Would turn and smile at me;
For he'd milk seven in the race
    While I was milking three.

He kissed me twice and once again
    And rode across the hill,
The pint-pots and the hobble-chain
    I hear them jingling still . . .
About the hut the sunlight fails,
    The fire shines through the cracks—
I climb the broken stockyard rails
    And watch the bridle-tracks.

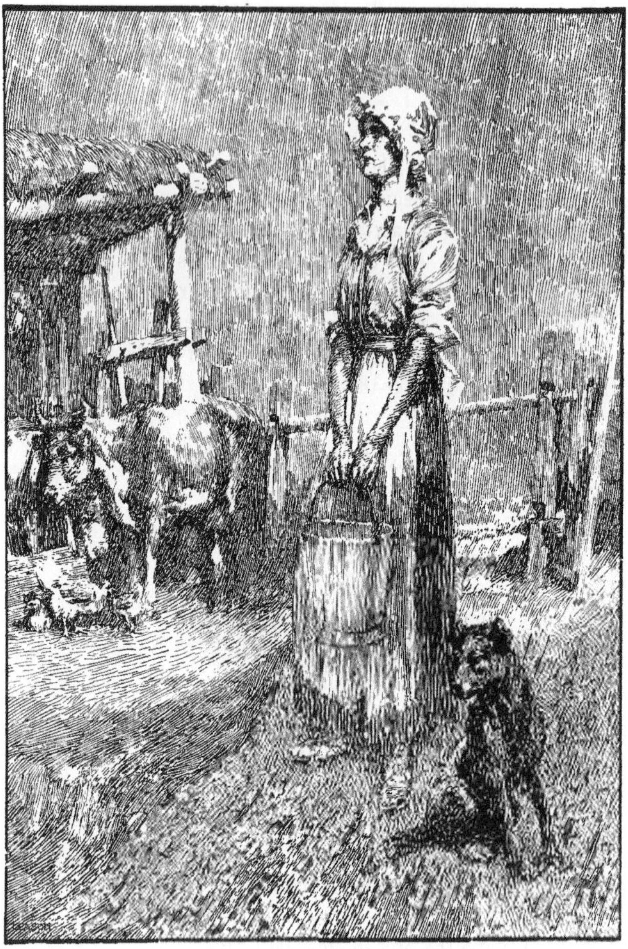

THE DROVER'S SWEETHEART

And he is coming back again—
   He wrote from Evatt's Rock;
A flood was in the Darling then
   And foot-rot in the flock.
The sheep were falling thick and fast
   A hundred miles from town,
And when he reached the line at last
   He trucked the remnant down.

And so he'll have to stand the cost;
   His luck was always bad,
Instead of making more, he lost
   The money that he had;
And how he'll manage, Heaven knows
   (My eyes are getting dim)
He says—he says—he don't—suppose
   I'll want—to—marry—him.

As if I wouldn't take his hand
   Without a golden glove—
Oh! Jack, you men won't understand
   How much a girl can love.
I long to see his face once more—
   Jack's dog! thank God, it's Jack!—
(I never thought I'd faint before)
   He's coming—up—the track.

1891

My Literary Friend

ONCE I wrote a little poem that I thought was very fine,
    And I showed the printer's copy to a critic friend of mine,
    First he praised the thing a little, then he found a little fault;
"The ideas are good," he muttered, "but the rhythm seems to halt."

So I straighten'd up the rhythm where he marked it with his pen,
And I copied it and showed it to my clever friend again.
"You've improved the metre greatly, but the rhymes are bad," he said
As he read it slowly, scratching surplus wisdom from his head.

So I worked as he suggested (I believe in taking time),
And I burnt the midnight taper while I straightened up the rhyme.
"It is better now," he muttered, "you go on and you'll succeed,
It has got a ring about it—the ideas are what you need."

So I worked for hours upon it (I go on when I commence)
And I kept in view the rhythm and the jingle and the sense,
And I copied it and took it to my solemn friend once more—
It reminded him of something he had somewhere read before!

  .   .   .   .

Now the people say I'd never put such horrors into print
If I wasn't too conceited to accept a friendly hint,
And my dearest friends are certain that I'd profit in the end
If I'd always show my copy to a literary friend.

1891

Ballad of the Rouseabout

A ROUSEABOUT of rouseabouts, from any land—
or none—
I bear a nickname of the Bush, and I'm—a woman's
son;
I came from where I camped last night, and at the
day-dawn glow
I'll rub the darkness from my eyes, roll up my swag, and go.

Some take the track for bitter pride, some for no pride at all—
(But to us all the world is wide when driven to the wall)
Some take the track for gain in life, some take the track for loss—
And some of us take up the swag as Christ took up the Cross.

Some take the track for faith in men—some take the track for
doubt—
Some flee a squalid home to work their own salvation out.
Some dared not see a mother's tears nor meet a father's face—
Born of good Christian families some leap, headlong, from Grace.

Oh, we are men who fought and rose, or fell from many grades;
Some born to lie, and some to pray, we're men of many trades;
We're men whose fathers were and are of high and low degree—
The sea was open to us, and we sailed across the sea.

We're haunted by the Past at times—and this is very bad,
Because we drink till horrors come, lest, sober, we go mad.
We judge not and we are not judged—'tis our philosophy;
There's something wrong with every ship that sails upon the sea.

BALLAD OF THE ROUSEABOUT

From shearing-shed to shearing-shed we tramp to make a cheque—
Jack Cornstalk and the Ne'er-do-well—the Tar-boy and the Wreck.
We know the tucker tracks that feed—or leave one in the lurch—
The "Burgoo" (Presbyterian) track—the "Murphy" (Roman Church).

I've humped my swag to Bawley Plain, and farther out and on;
I've boiled my billy by the Gulf, and boiled it by the Swan;
I've thirsted in dry lignum swamps, and thirsted on the sand,
And eked the fire with camel dung in Never-Never Land.

I've tramped, and camped, and "shore" and drunk with many mates Out Back—
And every one to me is Jack because the first was Jack—
A lifer sneaked from gaol at home—the straightest mate I met—
A ratty Russian Nihilist—a British Baronet!

A rouseabout of rouseabouts, above—beneath regard,
I know how soft is this old world, and I have learnt how hard—
I learned what college had to teach, and in the school of men
By camp-fires I have learned, or, say, unlearned it all again.

We hold him true who's true to one however false he be
(There's something wrong with every ship that lies beside the quay);
We lend and borrow, laugh and joke, and when the past is drowned
We sit upon our swags and smoke and watch the world go round.

1902

Andy's Gone With Cattle

OUR Andy's gone with cattle now—
    Our hearts are out of order—
With Drought he's gone to battle now
    Across the Queensland border.

He's left us in dejection now;
    Our thoughts with him are roving;
It's dull on this selection now,
    Since Andy went a-droving.

Who now shall wear the cheerful face
    In times when things are slackest?
And who shall whistle round the place
    When Fortune frowns her blackest?

Oh, who shall cheek the squatter now
    When he comes round us snarling?
His tongue is growing hotter now
    Since Andy cross'd the Darling.

Oh, may the showers in torrents fall,
    And all the tanks run over;
And may the grass grow green and tall
    In pathways of the drover;

And may good angels send the rain
    On desert stretches sandy;
And when the summer comes again
    God grant 'twill bring us Andy.

1888

The Vanguard

THEY say, in all kindness, I'm out of the hunt—
Too old and too deaf to be sent to the Front.
A scribbler of stories, a maker of songs,
To the fireside and armchair my valour belongs.
*Yet in hopeless campaigns and in bitterest strife
I have been at the Front all the days of my life.*

Oh, your girl feels a princess, your people are proud,
As you march down the street to the cheers of the crowd;
And the Nation's behind you and cloudless your sky,
And you come back to Honour, or gloriously die;
*But for each thing that brightens, and each thing that cheers,
I have starved in the trenches these forty long years.*

1915

Bill

HE shall live to the end of this mad, old world, he has
    lived since the world began,
    He never has done any good for himself, but was good
        to every man.
    He never has done any good for himself, and I'm sure
        that he never will;
He drinks and he swears, and he fights at times, and his name is
    mostly Bill.

He carried a freezing mate to his cave, and nursed him, for all I
    know,
When Europe was mostly a sheet of ice, thousands of years
    ago.
He has stuck to many a mate since then, he is with us every-
    where still
(He loves and gambles when he is young, and the girls stick up
    for Bill).

He has rowed to a wreck, when the life-boat failed, with Jim in
    a crazy boat;
He has given his lifebelt many a time, and sunk that another
    might float.
He has "stood 'em off" while others escaped, when the niggers
    rushed from the hill,
And rescue parties who came too late have found what was left
    of Bill.

He has thirsted on deserts that others might drink, he has given lest others should lack,
He has staggered half-blinded through fire or drought with a sick man on his back.
He is first to the rescue in tunnel or shaft, from Bulli to Broken Hill,
When the water breaks in or the fire breaks out, a leader of men is Bill!

He wears no Humane Society's badge for the fearful deaths he braved;
He seems ashamed of the good he did, and ashamed of the lives he saved.
If you chance to know of a noble deed he has done, you had best keep still;
If you chance to know of a kindly act, you mustn't let on to Bill.

He is fierce at a wrong, he is firm in right, he is kind to the weak and mild;
He will slave all day and sit up all night by the side of a neighbour's child.
For a woman in trouble he'd lay down his life, nor think as another man will;
He's a man all through, and no other man's wife has ever been worse for Bill.

He is good for the noblest sacrifice, he can do what few men can;
He will break his heart that the girl he loves may marry a better man.
There's many a mother and wife to-night whose heart and eyes will fill
When she thinks of the days of the long-ago when she well might have stuck to Bill.

Maybe he's in trouble or hard up now, and travelling far for work,
Or fighting a dead past down to-night in a lone camp west of Bourke.
When he's happy and flush, take your sorrow to him and borrow as much as you will;
But when he's in trouble or stony-broke, you never will hear from Bill.

And when, because of its million sins, this earth is cracked like a shell,
He will stand by a mate at the Judgment-Seat!—and comfort him down in—Well,
I haven't much sentiment left to waste, but let cynics sneer as they will,
Perhaps God will fix up the world again for the sake of the likes of Bill.

1905

When Your Pants Begin To Go

WHEN you wear a cloudy collar and a shirt that isn't
         white,
    And you cannot sleep for thinking how you'll reach
         to-morrow night,
    You may be a man of sorrow, and on speaking terms
         with Care,
But as yet you're unacquainted with the Demon of Despair;
For I rather think that nothing heaps the trouble on your mind
Like the knowledge that your trousers badly need a patch behind.

I have noticed when misfortune strikes the hero of the play
That his clothes are worn and tattered in a most unlikely way;
And the gods applaud and cheer him while he whines and loafs
    around,
But they never seem to notice that his pants are mostly sound;
Yet, of course, he cannot help it, for our mirth would mock his
    care
If the ceiling of his trousers showed the patches of repair.

You are none the less a hero if you elevate your chin
When you feel the pavement wearing through the leather, sock
    and skin;
You are rather more heroic than are ordinary folk
If you scorn to fish for pity under cover of a joke;
You will face the doubtful glances of the people that you know;
But—of course, you're bound to face them when your pants
    begin to go.

WHEN YOUR PANTS BEGIN TO GO

If, when flush, you took your pleasure—failed to make a god of
    Pelf—
Some will say that for your troubles you can only thank yourself;
Some will swear you'll die a beggar, but you only laugh at that
While your garments hang together and you wear a decent hat;
You may laugh at their predictions while your soles are wearing
    through—
But a man's an awful coward when his pants are going too!

Though the present and the future may be anything but bright,
It is best to tell the fellows that you're getting on all right.
And a man prefers to say it—'tis a manly lie to tell,
For the folks may be persuaded that you're doing very well;
But it's hard to be a hero, and it's hard to wear a grin,
When your most important garment is in places very thin.

Get some sympathy and comfort from the chum who knows you
    best,
Then your sorrows won't run over in the presence of the rest;
There's a chum that you can go to when you feel inclined to
    whine,
He'll declare your coat is tidy, and he'll say: "Just look at mine!"
Though you may be patched all over he will say it doesn't show,
And he'll swear it can't be noticed when your pants begin to go.

Brother mine, and of misfortune! times are hard, but do not fret,
Keep your courage up and struggle, and we'll laugh at these
    things yet.
Though there is no corn in Egypt, surely Africa has some—
Keep your smile in working order for the better days to come!
We shall often laugh together at the hard times that we know,
And get measured by the tailor when our pants begin to go.

1892

The Teams

A CLOUD of dust on the long, white road,
    And the teams go creeping on
Inch by inch with the weary load;
And by the power of the green-hide goad
    The distant goal is won.

With eyes half-shut to the blinding dust,
    And necks to the yokes bent low,
The beasts are pulling as bullocks must;
And the shining tires might almost rust
    While the spokes are turning slow.

With face half-hid by a broad-brimmed hat,
    That shades from the heat's white waves,
And shouldered whip, with its green-hide plait,
The driver plods with a gait like that
    Of his weary, patient slaves.

He wipes his brow, for the day is hot,
    And spits to the left with spite;
He shouts at Bally, and flicks at Scot,
And raises dust from the back of Spot,
    And spits to the dusty right.

He'll sometimes pause as a thing of form
    In front of a settler's door,
And ask for a drink, and remark "It's warm,"
Or say "There's signs of a thunderstorm";
    But he seldom utters more.

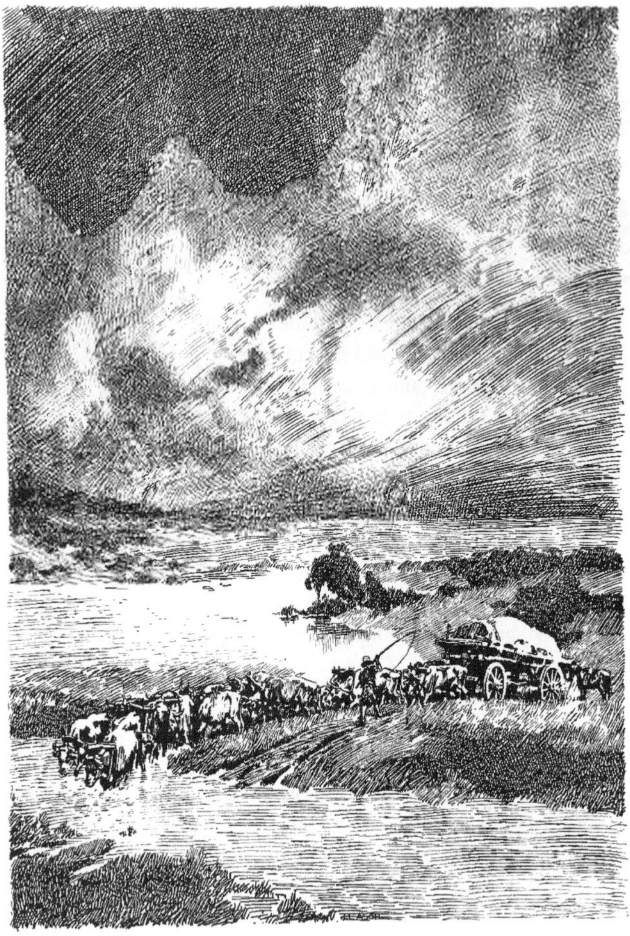

THE TEAMS

The rains are heavy on roads like these
   And, fronting his lonely home,
For days together the settler sees
The waggons bogged to the axletrees,
   Or ploughing the sodden loam.

And then, when the roads are at their worst,
   The bushman's children hear
The cruel blows of the whips reversed
While bullocks pull as their hearts would burst,
   And bellow with pain and fear.

And thus—with glimpses of home and rest—
   Are the long, long journeys done;
And thus—'tis a thankless life at the best!—
Is Distance fought in the mighty West,
   And the lonely battle won.

1889

When the World was Wide

THE world is narrow and ways are short, and our
    lives are dull and slow,
  For little is new where the crowds resort, and less
    where the wanderers go;
  Greater or smaller, the same old things we see by the
    dull roadside—
And tired of all is the spirit that sings of the days when the
  world was wide.

When the North was hale in the march of Time, and the South
  and the West were new,
And the gorgeous East was a pantomime, as it seemed in our
  boyhood's view;
When Spain was first on the waves of change, and proud in the
  ranks of pride,
And all was wonderful, new and strange in the days when the
  world was wide.

Then a man could fight if his heart were bold, and win if his
  faith were true—
Were it love, or honour, or power, or gold, or all that our hearts
  pursue;
Could live to the world for the family name, or die for the family
  pride,
Could fly from sorrow, and wrong and shame in the days when
  the world was wide.

They sailed away in the ships that sailed ere science controlled
    the main,
When the strong, brave heart of a man prevailed as 'twill never
    prevail again;
They knew not whither, nor much they cared—let Fate or the
    winds decide—
The worst of the Great Unknown they dared in the days when
    the world was wide.

They raised new stars on the silent sea that filled their hearts
    with awe;
They came to many a strange countree and marvellous sights
    they saw.
The villagers gaped at the tales they told, and old eyes glistened
    with pride—
When barbarous cities were paved with gold in the days when
    the world was wide.

'Twas honest metal and honest wood, in the days of the Outward
    Bound,
When men were gallant and ships were good—roaming the wide
    world round.
The gods could envy a leader then when "Follow me, lads!" he
    cried—
They faced each other and fought like men in the days when
    the world was wide!

They tried to live as a freeman should—they were happier men
    than we,
In the glorious days of wine and blood, when Liberty crossed
    the sea;
'Twas a comrade true or a foeman then, and a trusty sword
    well-tried—
They faced each other and fought like men in the days when
    the world was wide.

The good ship bound for the Southern Seas when the beacon was Ballarat,
With a "Ship ahoy!" on the freshening breeze, "Where bound?" and "What ship's that?"—
The emigrant train to New Mexico—the rush to the Lachlan-side—
Ah! faint is the echo of Westward Ho! from the days when the world was wide.

South, East, and West in advance of Time—and far in advance of Thought—
Brave men they were with a faith sublime—and is it for this they fought?
And is it for this damned life we praise the god-like spirit that died
At Eureka Stockade in the Roaring Days with the days when the world was wide?

We fight like women, and feel as much; the thoughts of our hearts we guard;
Where scarcely the scorn of a god could touch, the sneer of the sneak hits hard;
The treacherous tongue and cowardly pen, the weapons of curs, decide—
They faced each other and fought like men in the days when the world was wide.

Think of it all—of the life that is! Study your friends and foes!
Study the Past! and answer this: "Are these times better than those?"
The life-long quarrel, the paltry spite, the sting of your poisoned pride!
No matter who fell, it were better to fight as they did when the world was wide.

Boast as you will of your mateship now—crippled and mean and sly—
The lines of suspicion on friendship's brow were traced since the days gone by.
There was room in the long, free lines of the van to fight for it side by side—
There was beating-room for the heart of a man in the days when the world was wide.

. . . .

With its dull, brown days of a-shilling-an-hour the dreary year drags round:
Is this the result of Old England's power?—the bourne of the Outward Bound?
Is this the sequel of Westward Ho!—of the days of Whate'er Betide?
The heart of the rebel makes answer "No! We'll fight till the world grows wide!"

The world shall yet be a wider world—for the tokens are manifest;
East and North shall the wrongs be hurled that followed us South and West.
The march of Freedom is North by the Dawn! Follow, whate'er betide!
Sons of the Exiles, march! March on! March till the world grows wide!

1896

Ballad of the Elder Son

A SON of elder sons am I
    Whose boyhood days were cramped and scant:
Who lived the old domestic lie
    And breathed the old familiar cant.
Come, elder brothers mine, and bring
    Dull loads of care that you have won,
And gather round me while I sing
    The ballad of the elder son.

The elder son on barren soil,
    Where life is crude and lands are new,
Must share the father's hardest toil,
    And see the father's troubles through.
With no child-thoughts to match his own,
    No game to play, no race to run,
The youth his father might have known
    Is seldom for the elder son.

. . .

A certain squatter had two sons
    Up Canaan way some years ago.
The graft was hard on those old runs.
    And it was hot and life was slow.
The younger brother coolly claimed
    The portion that he hadn't earned,
And sought the "life" for which untamed
    And high young spirits always yearned.

BALLAD OF THE ELDER SON

A year or so he knocked about,
   And spent his cheques on girls and wine,
And, getting stony in the drought,
   He took a job at herding swine;
And though he was a hog to swig,
   And fool with girls till all was blue—
'Twas rather rough to mind the pig
   And have to eat its tucker too.

But coming to himself, he said—
   He reckoned shrewdly, though dead beat—
"The rousers in my father's shed
   Have got more grub than they can eat;
I've been a fool, but such is fate—
   I guess I'll talk the guv'nor round:
'I've acted cronk,' I'll tell him straight;
   (He's had his time, too, I'll be bound).

"I'll tell him straight I've had my fling,
   I'll tell him 'I've been on the beer,
But put me on at anything,
   I'll graft with any bounder here.' "
He rolled his swag and struck for home,
   (By this time he was pretty slim),
And, when the old man saw him come—
   Well, you know how he welcomed him.

They've brought the best robe in the house,
   The ring, and killed the fatted calf,
And now they hold a grand carouse,
   And eat and drink and dance and laugh:
And from the field the elder son—
   Whose character is not admired—
Comes plodding home when work is done,
   Extremely hot and very tired.

BALLAD OF THE ELDER SON

He asked the meaning of the sound
   Of such unwonted revelry,
They said his brother had been "found"
   (He'd found himself, it seems to me);
'Twas natural the elder son
   Should take the thing a little hard
And brood on what was past and done
   While standing, pensive, in the yard.

Now, he was hungry and knocked out
   And would, if they had let him be,
Have rested and cooled down, no doubt,
   And hugged his brother after tea
And welcomed him, and hugged his dad,
   And filled the wine-cup to the brim—
But, just when he was feeling bad,
   The old man came and tackled him.

He well might say with bitter tears
   While music swelled and flowed the wine—
"Lo, I have served thee many years
   Nor caused thee one grey hair of thine.
Whate'er thou bad'st me do I did
   And for my brother made amends;
Thou never gavest me a kid
   For merry-making with my friends."

(He was no heavy clod and glum
   Who could not trespass, sing or dance—
He could be merry with a chum,
   It seemed, if he had half a chance;
Perhaps, if further light we seek,
   He knew—and herein lay the sting—
His brother would clear out next week
   And promptly pop the robe and ring.)

BALLAD OF THE ELDER SON

The father said, "The wandering one,
   The lost is found, this son of mine,
But thou art always with me, son—
   Thou knowest all I have is thine."
(It seemed the best robe and the ring,
   The love and fatted calf were not;
But this was just a little thing
   The old man in his joy forgot.)

   .   .   .   .

Oh! if I had the power to teach—
   The strength for which my spirit craves—
The cant of parents I would preach
   Who slave and make their children slaves.
For greed of gain, and that alone,
   Their youth they steal, their hearts they break;
And then the wretched misers moan—
   "We did it for our children's sake."

"And all I have"—the paltry bribe
   That he might slave contented yet,
While envied by his selfish tribe
   The birthright he might never get:
The worked-out farm and endless graft,
   The mortgaged home, the barren run—
The heavy, hopeless overdraft—
   The portion of the elder son.

He keeps his parents when they're old,
   He keeps a sister in distress,
His wife must work and care for them
   And bear with all their pettishness.

BALLAD OF THE ELDER SON

The mother's moan is ever heard,
    And, whining for the worthless one,
She seldom has a kindly word
    To say about her eldest son.

'Tis he, in spite of sneer and jibe,
    Who stands the friend when others fail:
He bears the burdens of his tribe
    And keeps his brother out of jail.
He lends the quid and pays the fine,
    And for the family pride he smarts—
For reasons I can not divine
    They hate him in their heart of hearts.

Sometimes the Eldest takes the track
    When things at home have got too bad—
He comes not crawling, canting back
    To seek the blind side of his dad.
He always finds a knife and fork
    And meat between on which to dine,
And, though he sometimes deals in pork,
    He never eats his meals with swine.

The happy home, the overdraft,
    His birthright and his prospects gay,
And likewise his share of the graft,
    He leaves the rest to grab. And they—
Who'd always do the thing by halves,
    If anything for him was done—
Should kill a score of fatted calves
    To welcome home the eldest son.

1904

The Southerly Buster

THERE'S a wind that blows out of the South in
    the drought,
And we pray for the touch of his breath
When siroccos come forth from the Nor'-West
    and North,
    Or in dead calms of fever and death.
With eyes glad and dim we should sing him a hymn,
    For depression and death are his foes;
Oh, it gives us new life for the bread-winning strife
    When the glorious Old Southerly blows.

Old Southerly Buster! your forces you muster
    Where seldom a wind bloweth twice,
And your white-caps have hint of the snow caps, and glint of
    The far-away barriers of ice.
No wind the wide sea on can sing such a pæan,
    Or do the great work that you do;
Our Own Wind and Only, from seas wild and lonely—
    Old Southerly Buster!—To you!

Oh, the city is baked, and our thirst is unslaked
    Though we swallow iced drinks by the score,
And the blurred sky is low, and the air seems aglow
    As if breezes would cool it no more.
But we watch from The Shore (and a few places more)—
    And we're looking out hopefully, too—
For a red light shall glower from the Post Office tower
    When the Southerly Buster is due.

THE SOUTHERLY BUSTER

The yachts cut away at the close of the day
   From the breakers commencing to comb,
For a few he may swamp in the health-giving romp
   With the friendly Old Southerly home.
Oh, softly he plays through the city's hot ways
   To the beds where they're calling "Come, quick!"
He is gentle and mild round the feverish child,
   And he cools the hot brow of the sick.

'Tis a glorious mission, Old Sydney's Physician!—
   Broom, Bucket, and Cloth of the East!
'Tis a breeze and a sprayer that answers our prayer,
   And it's free to the greatest and least.
The red-lamp's a warning to drought and its scorning—
   A sign to the city at large—
Hence, Headache and Worry! Despondency, hurry!
   Old Southerly Buster's in charge.

Old Southerly Buster! your forces you muster
   Where seldom a wind bloweth twice,
And your white-caps have hint of the snow caps, and glint of
   The far-away barriers of ice.
No wind the wide sea on can sing such a pæan,
   Or do the great work that you do;
Our Own Wind and Only, from seas wild and lonely—
   Old Southerly Buster!—To you!

(1910)

Out Back

THE old year went, and the new returned, in the withering weeks of drought,
The cheque was spent that the shearer earned, and the sheds were all cut out;
The publican's words were short and few, and the publican's looks were black—
And the time had come, as the shearer knew, to carry his swag Out Back.

For time means tucker, and tramp you must, where the scrubs and plains are wide,
With seldom a track that a man can trust, or a mountain peak to guide;
All day long in the dust and heat—when summer is on the track—
With stinted stomachs and blistered feet, they carry their swags Out Back.

He tramped away from the shanty there, when the days were long and hot,
With never a soul to know or care if he died on the track or not.
The poor of the city have friends in woe, no matter how much they lack,
But only God and the swagmen know how a poor man fares Out Back.

He begged his way on the parched Paroo and the Warrego tracks
  once more,
And lived like a dog, as the swagmen do, till the Western stations
  shore:
But men were many, and sheds were full, for work in the town
  was slack—
The traveller never got hands in wool, though he tramped for a
  year Out Back.

In stifling noons when his back was wrung by its load, and the
  air seemed dead,
And the water warmed in the bag that hung to his aching arm
  like lead,
Or in times of flood, when plains were seas, and the scrubs were
  cold and black,
He ploughed in mud to his trembling knees, and paid for his
  sins Out Back.

He blamed himself in the year "Too Late," for the wreck of
  his strong young life,
And no one knew but a shearing mate 'twas the fault of his
  faithless wife.
When the wrongs of your kindred bid you roam, and treacherous
  tongues attack,
It is best that a man be far from home, and dead to the world,
  Out Back.

And dirty and careless and old he wore, as his lamp of hope
  grew dim;
He tramped for years till the swag he bore seemed part of himself to him.
As a bullock drags in the sandy ruts, he followed the dreary
  track,
With never a thought but to reach the huts when the sun went
  down Out Back.

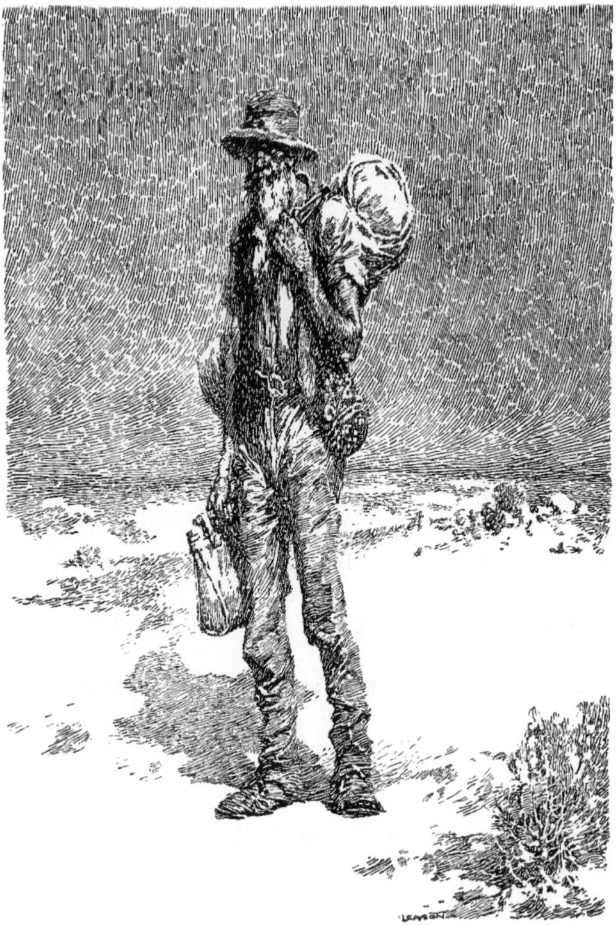

OUT BACK

It chanced one day when the north wind blew in his face like a furnace-breath,
He left the track for a tank he knew—'twas a shorter cut to death;
For the bed of the tank was hard and dry, and crossed with many a crack,
And, oh! it's a terrible thing to die of thirst in the scrub Out Back.

A drover came, but the fringe of law was eastward many a mile;
He never reported the thing he saw, for it was not worth his while.
The tanks are full, and the grass is high in the mulga off the track,
Where the bleaching bones of a white man lie by his mouldering swag Out Back.

For time means tucker, and tramp they must, where the plains and scrubs are wide,
With seldom a track that a man can trust, or a mountain peak to guide;
All day long in the flies and heat the men of the outside track,
With stinted stomachs and blistered feet, must carry their swags Out Back.

1893

Ballad of the Drover

ACROSS the stony ridges,
   Across the rolling plain,
Young Harry Dale, the drover,
   Comes riding home again.
And well his stock-horse bears him,
   And light of heart is he,
And stoutly his old packhorse
   Is trotting by his knee.

Up Queensland way with cattle
   He's travelled regions vast,
And many months have vanished
   Since home-folk saw him last.
He hums a song of someone
   He hopes to marry soon;
And hobble-chains and camp-ware
   Keep jingling to the tune.

Beyond the hazy dado
   Against the lower skies
And yon blue line of ranges
   The homestead station lies.
And thitherward the drover
   Jogs through the lazy noon,
While hobble-chains and camp-ware
   Are jingling to a tune.

BALLAD OF THE DROVER

An hour has filled the heavens
   With storm-clouds inky black;
At times the lightning trickles
   Around the drover's track;
But Harry pushes onward,
   His horses' strength he tries,
In hope to reach the river
   Before the flood shall rise.

The thunder pealing o'er him
   Goes rumbling down the plain;
And sweet on thirsty pastures
   Beats fast the plashing rain;
Then every creek and gully
   Sends forth its tribute flood—
The river runs a banker,
   All stained with yellow mud.

Now Harry speaks to Rover,
   The best dog on the plains,
And to his hardy horses,
   And strokes their shaggy manes:
"We've breasted bigger rivers
   When floods were at their height
Nor shall this gutter stop us
   From getting home to-night!"

The thunder growls a warning,
   The blue, forked lightnings gleam;
The drover turns his horses
   To swim the fatal stream.
But, oh! the flood runs stronger
   Than e'er it ran before;
The saddle-horse is failing,
   And only half-way o'er!

When flashes next the lightning,
  The flood's grey breast is blank;
A cattle dog and packhorse
  Are struggling up the bank.
But in the lonely homestead
  The girl shall wait in vain—
He'll never pass the stations
  In charge of stock again.

The faithful dog a moment
  Lies panting on the bank,
Then plunges through the current
  To where his master sank.
And round and round in circles
  He fights with failing strength,
Till, gripped by wilder waters,
  He fails and sinks at length.

Across the flooded lowlands
  And slopes of sodden loam
The packhorse struggles bravely
  To take dumb tidings home;
And mud-stained, wet, and weary,
  He goes by rock and tree,
With clanging chains and tinware
  All sounding eerily.

1889

After All

THE brooding ghosts of Australian night have gone
from the bush and town;
My spirit revives in the morning breeze, though it
died when the sun went down;
The river is high and the stream is strong, and the
grass is green and tall,
And I fain would think that this world of ours is a good world
after all.

The light of passion in dreamy eyes, and a page of truth well
read,
The glorious thrill, in a heart grown cold, of the spirit I thought
was dead,
A song that goes to a comrade's heart, and a tear of pride let
fall—
And my soul is strong! and the world to me is a grand world
after all!

Let our enemies go by their old dull tracks, and theirs be the fault
or shame
(The man is bitter against the world who has only himself to
blame);
Let the darkest side of the past be dark, and only the good recall;
For I must believe that the world, my dear, is a kind world after
all.

It well may be that I saw too plain, and it may be I was blind;
But I'll keep my face to the dawning light, though the devil may
stand behind!

Though the devil may stand behind my back, shall I see his
    shadow fall?
I'll read in the light of the morning stars—a good world after all.

Rest, for your eyes are weary, girl,—you have driven the worst
    away;—
The ghost of the man that I might have been is gone from my
    heart to-day;
We'll live for life and the best it brings till our twilight shadows
    fall;
My heart grows brave, and the world, my girl, is a good world
    after all.

1896

Black Bonnet

A DAY of seeming innocence,
    A glorious sun and sky,
And, just above my picket fence,
    Black Bonnet passing by.
In knitted gloves and quaint old dress,
    Without a spot or smirch,
Her worn face lit with peacefulness,
    Old Granny goes to church.

Her hair is richly white, like milk,
    That long ago was fair—
And glossy still the old black silk
    She keeps for "chapel wear";
Her bonnet, of a bygone style
    That long has passed away,
She must have kept a weary while
    Just as it is to-day.

The parasol of days gone by—
    Old days that seemed the best—
The hymn and prayer books carried high
    Against her warm, thin breast;
As she had clasped—come smiles come tears,
    Come hardship, aye, and worse—
On market days, through faded years,
    The slender household purse.

BLACK BONNET

Although the road is rough and steep,
    She takes it with a will,
For, since she hushed her first to sleep
    Her way has been uphill.
Instinctively I bare my head
    (A sinful one, alas!)
Whene'er I see, by church bells led,
    Brave Old Black Bonnet pass.

For she has known the cold and heat
    And dangers of the Track:
Has fought bush-fires to save the wheat
    And little home Out Back.
By barren creeks the Bushman loves,
    In stockyard, hut, and pen,
The withered hands in those old gloves
    Have done the work of men.

.   .   .   .   .

They called it "Service" long ago
    When Granny yet was young,
And in the chapel, sweet and low,
    As girls her daughters sung.
And when in church she bends her head
    (But not as others do)
She sees her loved ones, and her dead,
    And hears their voices too.

Fair as the Saxons in her youth,
    Not forward, and not shy;
And strong in healthy life and truth
    As after years went by:

BLACK BONNET

She often laughed with sinners vain,
    Yet passed from faith to sight—
God gave her beauty back again
    The more her hair grew white.

She came out in the Early Days,
    (Green seas, and blue—and grey)—
The village fair, and English ways,
    Seemed worlds and worlds away.
She fought the haunting loneliness
    Where brooding gum trees stood;
And won through sickness and distress
    As Englishwomen could.

   .   .   .   .   .

By verdant swath and ivied wall
    The congregation's seen—
White nothings where the shadows fall,
    Black blots against the green.
The dull, suburban people meet
    And buzz in little groups,
While down the white steps to the street
    A quaint old figure stoops.

And then along my picket fence
    Where staring wallflowers grow—
World-wise Old Age, and Common-sense!—
    Black Bonnet, nodding slow.
But not alone; for on each side
    A little dot attends
In snowy frock and sash of pride,
    And these are Granny's friends.

To them her mind is clear and bright,
    Her old ideas are new;
They know her "real talk" is right,
    Her "fairy talk" is true.
And they converse as grown-ups may,
    When all the news is told;
The one so wisely young to-day,
    The two so wisely old.

At home, with dinner waiting there,
    She smooths her hair and face,
And puts her bonnet by with care
    And dons a cap of lace.
The table minds its p's and q's
    Lest one perchance be hit
By some rare dart which is a part
    Of her old-fashioned wit.

    .   .   .   .   .

Her son and son's wife are asleep,
    She puts her apron on—
The quiet house is hers to keep,
    With all the youngsters gone.
There's scarce a sound of dish on dish
    Or cup slipped into cup,
When left alone, as is her wish,
    Black Bonnet "washes up!"

1916

My Army, O My Army!

MY army, O my army! The time I dreamed of comes!
I want to see your colours; I long to hear your drums!
I heard them in my boyhood when all men's hearts seemed cold;
I heard them through the Years of Life—and now I'm growing old!
My army, O my army! The signs are manifold!

My army, O my army! My army and my Queen!
I sang your Southern battle-songs when I was seventeen!
They echoed down the Ages, they came from far and near;
They came to me from Paris, they came to me from Here!—
They came while I was marching with the Army of the Rear.

My Queen's dark eyes were flashing (oh, she was younger then!)
My Queen's Red Cap was redder than the reddest blood of men!
My Queen marched like an Amazon, with anger manifest—
Her wild hair darkly matted from a knife-gash in her breast
(For blood will flow where milk will not—her sisters knew the rest).

My legions ne'er were listed, they had no need to be;
My army ne'er was trained to arms—'twas trained to misery!
It took long years to mould it, but war could never drown
The shuffling of my army's feet at drill in Hunger Town—
A little child was murdered, and so Tyranny went down.

MY ARMY, O MY ARMY

My army kept no order, my army kept no time;
My army dug no trenches, yet died in dust and slime;
Its troops were fiercely ignorant, as to the manner born;
Its clothes were rags and tatters—patched rags, the patches torn—
Ah, me! It wore a uniform that I have often worn.

The faces of my army were ghastly as the dead;
My army's cause was Hunger, my army's cry was "Bread!"
It called on God and Mary and Christ of Nazareth;
It cried to kings and courtesans that fainted at its breath—
Its women beat their poor, flat breasts where babes had starved to death.

. . . .

My army! O my army—I hear the sound of drums
Above the roar of battle—and, lo, my army comes!
Nor creed of man may stay it—nor war, nor nations' law—
Ho, Fan of God that blows the chaff! Ho, Flames amid the straw!
The world shall burn in hells it made to keep the poor in awe!

1915

Talbragar

JACK DENVER died on Talbragar when Christmas
      Eve began,
And there was sorrow round the place, for Denver
      was a man;
Jack Denver's wife bowed down her head—her
      daughter's grief was wild,
And big Ben Duggan by the bed stood sobbing like a child.
But big Ben Duggan saddled up, and galloped fast and far,
To raise the biggest funeral yet seen on Talbragar.
      By station home
      And shearing shed
      Ben Duggan cried, "Jack Denver's dead!
      Roll up at Talbragar!"

He borrowed horses here and there, and rode all Christmas Eve,
And scarcely paused a moment's time the mournful news to
      leave;
He rode by lonely huts and farms until the day was done,
And then he turned his horse's head and made for Ross's Run.
No bushman in a single day had ridden half so far
Since Johnson brought the doctor to his wife at Talbragar.
      By diggers' camps
      Ben Duggan sped—
      At each he cried, "Jack Denver's dead!
      Roll up at Talbragar!"

That night he passed the humpies of the splitters on the ridge,
And roused the bullock-drivers camped at Belinfante's Bridge;

And as he climbed the ridge again the moon shone on the rise—
Did moonbeams glisten in the mist of tears that filled his eyes?
He dashed the rebel drops away—for blinding things they are—
But 'twas his best and truest friend who died on Talbragar.
   At Blackman's Run
   Before the dawn
   Ben Duggan cried, "Jack Denver's gone!
   Roll up at Talbragar!"

At all the shanties round the place they heard his horse's tramp,
He took the track to Wilson's Luck, and told the diggers' camp;
But in the gorge by Deadman's Gap the mountain shades were
  black,
And there a newly-fallen tree was lying on the track—
He saw too late, and then he heard the swift hoof's sudden jar,
And big Ben Duggan ne'er again rode home to Talbragar.
   "The wretch is drunk,
   And Denver's dead—
   A burning shame!" the people said
   Next day at Talbragar.

For thirty miles round Talbragar the boys rolled up in strength,
And Denver had a funeral a good long mile in length;
Round Denver's grave that Christmas Day rough Bushmen's
  eyes were dim—
The Western Bushmen knew the way to bury dead like him;
But some returning homeward found, by light of moon and star,
Ben Duggan lying in the rocks, five miles from Talbragar.
   And far and wide
   When Duggan died,
   The bushmen of the western side
   Rode in to Talbragar.

1891

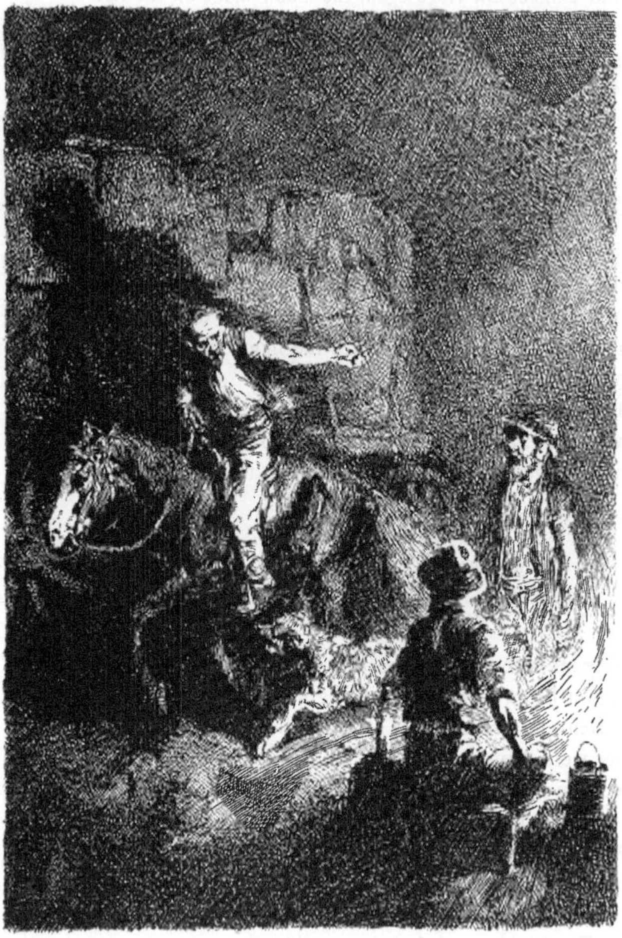

Above Crow's Nest

A BLANKET low and leaden,
   Though rent across the west,
Whose darkness seems to deaden
   The City to its rest;
A sunset white and staring
   On cloud-wrack far away—
And haggard house-walls glaring
   A farewell to the day.

A light on tower and steeple,
   Where sun no longer shines—
My people, O my people!
   Rise up and read the signs!
Low looms the nearer high-line
   (No sign of star or moon),
The Horseman on the skyline
   Rode hard this afternoon!

(Is he—and who shall know it?—
   The spectre of a scout?
Or spirit of a poet,
   Whose truths were met with doubt?
Who sought and who succeeded
   In marking danger's track—
Whose warnings were unheeded
   Till all the sky was black?)

ABOVE CROW'S NEST

Without the sacrifices
    That make a nation's name,
The elder nations' vices
    And luxuries we claim.
Without their rise and glory
    We fall like Greece and Rome!
It is a shameful story
    That men should tell at home.

Grown vain without a conquest,
    And sure without a fort,
And maddened in the one quest
    Of pleasure or of sport,
Self-blinded to our starkness
    We fling the time away—
To fight, half-armed, in darkness,
    Who should be armed to-day.

Cloud-fortresses titanic
    Along the western sky—
The tired, bowed mechanic
    And pallid clerk flit by.
Lit by a light unhealthy,
    The ghastly after-glare,
The veiled and goggled wealthy
    Drive fast—they know not where.

Night's sullen spirit rouses,
    The darkening gables lour,
From ugly four-roomed houses
    Verandah'd windows glower;
The last long day-stare dies on
    The scrub-ridged western side,
And round the near horizon
    The spectral horsemen ride.

1907

The Shakedown on the Floor

SET me back for twenty summers,
    For I'm tired of cities now—
Set my feet in red-soil furrows
    And my hands upon the plough,
With the two Black Brothers trudging
    On the home stretch through the loam—
While along the grassy sidling
    Come the cattle grazing home.

And I finish ploughing early,
    And I hurry home to tea—
There's my black suit on the stretcher,
    And a clean white shirt for me;
There's a dance at Rocky Rises,
    And, when they can dance no more,
For a certain favoured party
    There's a shakedown on the floor.

You remember Mary Carey,
    Bushmen's favourite at The Rise?
With her sweet small freckled features,
    Red-gold hair, and kind grey eyes;
Sister, daughter, to her mother,
    Mother, sister, to the rest—
And of all my friends and kindred
    Mary Carey loved me best.

THE SHAKEDOWN ON THE FLOOR

Far too shy, because she loved me,
  To be dancing oft with me;
(What cared I, because she loved me,
  If the world were there to see?)
But we lingered by the sliprails
  While the rest were riding home,
Ere the hour before the dawning
  Dimmed the great star-clustered dome.

Small brown hands that spread the mattress,
  While the old folk winked to see
How she'd find an extra pillow
  And an extra sheet for me.
For a moment shyly smiling,
  She would grant me one kiss more—
Slip away and leave me happy
  By the shakedown on the floor.

Rock me hard in steerage cabins,
  Rock me soft in first saloons,
Lay me on the sandhill lonely
  Under waning Western moons;
But wherever night may find me
  Till I rest for evermore—
I shall dream that I am happy
  In the shakedown on the floor.

(1900)

Written Afterwards

(To J. Le Gay Brereton)

SO the days of my riding are over,
    The days of my tramping are done—
I'm about as content as a rover
    Will ever be under the sun;
I write, after reading your letter—
    My mind with old memories rife—
And I feel in a mood that had better
    Not meet the true eyes of the wife.

You must never admit a suggestion
    That old things are good to recall;
You must never consider the question:
    "Was I happier then, after all?"
You must banish the old hope and sorrow
    That make the sad pleasures of life;
You must live for To-day and To-morrow
    If you want to be just to the wife.

I have changed since the first day I kissed her,
    Which is due—Heaven bless her!—to her;
I'm respected and trusted—I'm "Mister,"
    Addressed by the children as "Sir."
I feel the respect without feigning,
    And you'd laugh the great laugh of your life
If you only saw me entertaining
    An old lady friend of the wife.

WRITTEN AFTERWARDS

By the way, when you're writing, remember
   You never went drinking with me,
And forget our Last Nights of December,
   Lest our sev'ral accounts disagree.
And, for my sake, old man, you had better
   Avoid the old language of strife,
For the technical terms of your letter
   Will be misconstrued by the wife.

Never hint of the girls appertaining
   To the past, when you're writing again,
For they take such a lot of explaining—
   And you know how I hate to explain.
There are some things, we know to our sorrow,
   That cut to the heart like a knife,
And your past is To-day and To-morrow
   If you want to be true to the wife.

No doubt you are dreaming as I did
   And going the careless old pace,
But my future grows dull and decided,
   And the world narrows down to the Place.
Let it be. If my treason's resented,
   You may do worse, old man, in your life;
Let me dream, too, that I am contented—
   For the sake of a true little wife.

1898

The Green-hand Rouseabout

CALL this hot? I beg your pardon. Hot!—you don't
    know what it means.
(What's that, waiter? lamb or mutton! Thank you—
    mine is beef and greens.
Bread and butter while I'm waiting. Milk? Oh, yes—
    a bucketful.)
I'm just in from west the Darling, "picking-up" and "rolling
    wool."

Mutton stewed or chops for breakfast, dry and tasteless, boiled
    in fat;
Bread or brownie, tea or coffee—two hours' graft in front of
    that;
Legs of mutton boiled for dinner—mutton greasy-warm for tea—
Mutton curried (gave my order, beef and plenty greens for me.)
Breakfast, curried rice and mutton till your innards sacrifice,
And you sicken at the colour and the very look of rice.
All day long with living mutton—bits and belly-wool and fleece;
Blinded by the yoke of wool, and shirt and trousers stiff with
    grease,
Till you long for sight of verdure, cabbage-plots and water clear,
And you crave for beef and butter as a boozer craves for beer.

   .   .   .   .

Dusty patch in baking mulga—glaring iron hut and shed—
Feel and scent of rain forgotten—water scarce and feed-grass
    dead.

THE GREEN-HAND ROUSEABOUT

Hot and suffocating sunrise—all-pervading sheep-yard smell—
Stiff and aching, Greenhand stretches—"Slushy" rings the bullock-bell—
Pint of tea and hunk of brownie—sinners string towards the shed—
Great, black, greasy crows round carcass—screen behind of dust-cloud red.
Engine whistles. "Go it, tigers!" and the agony begins,
Picking up for seven shearers—rushing, sweating for my sins;
Picking up for seven demons, seven devils out of Hell!
Sell their souls to get the bell-sheep—half-a-dozen Christs they'd sell!
Day grows hot as where they come from—too damned hot for men or brutes;
Roof of corrugated iron, six-foot-six above the shoots!
Whiz and rattle and vibration, like an endless chain of trams;
Blasphemy of five-and-forty—prickly heat—and stink of rams!
Barcoo leaves his pen-door open and the sheep come bucking out;
When the rouser goes to pen them Barcoo blasts the rouseabout.
Injury with insult added—trial of our cursing powers—
Cursed and cursing back enough to damn a dozen worlds like ours.
"Take my combs down to the grinder!" "Seen my (something) cattle-pup?"
"There's a crawler down in my shoot—just slip through and pick it up."
"Give the office when the boss comes." "Catch that gory ram, old man."
"Count the sheep in my pen, will you?" "Fetch my combs back when you can."
"When you get a chance, old fellow, will you pop down to the hut?
Fetch my pipe—the cook 'll show you—and I'll let you have a cut."

Shearer yells for tar and needle. Ringer's roaring like a bull:
"Wool away, you (son of angels). Where the hell's the (foundling)? WOOL!"

. . . . . .

Pound a week and station prices—mustn't kick against the pricks—
Seven weeks of lurid mateship—ruined soul and four pounds six.

. . . . . .

What's that? Waiter! *Me?* Stuffed Mutton! Look here, waiter, to be brief,
I said beef! you blood-stained villain! Beef—moo-cow—Roast Bullock—BEEF!

1897

Scots of the Riverina

THE boy cleared out to the city from his home at the harvest time—
They were Scots of the Riverina, and to run from home was a crime.
The old man burned his letters, the first and last he burned,
And he scratched his name from the Bible when the old wife's back was turned.

A year went past and another. There were calls from the firing-line;
They heard the boy had enlisted, but the old man made no sign.
His name must never be mentioned on the farm by Gundagai—
They were Scots of the Riverina with ever the kirk hard by.

The boy came home on his "final," and the township's bonfire burned.
His mother's arms were about him; but the old man's back was turned.
The daughters begged for pardon till the old man raised his hand—
A Scot of the Riverina who was hard to understand.

The boy was killed in Flanders, where the best and bravest die.
There were tears at the Grahame homestead and grief in Gundagai;
But the old man ploughed at daybreak and the old man ploughed till the mirk—
There were furrows of pain in the orchard while his household went to the kirk.

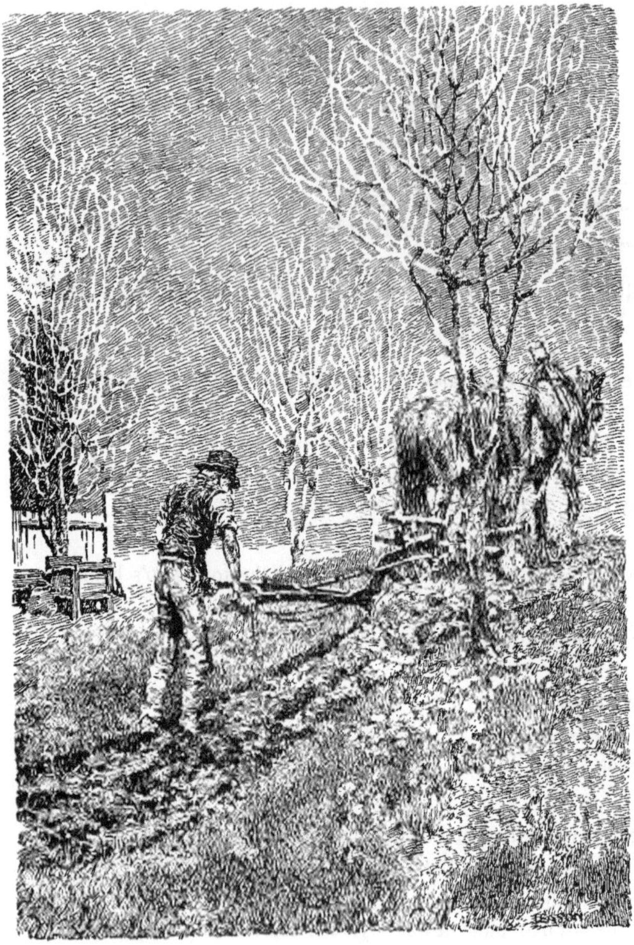

The Never-Never Land

BY homestead, hut, and shearing-shed,
    By railroad, coach, and track—
By lonely graves where rest our dead,
    Up-Country and Out-Back:
To where beneath the clustered stars
    The dreamy plains expand—
My home lies wide a thousand miles
    In the Never-Never Land.

It lies beyond the farming belt,
    Wide wastes of scrub and plain,
A blazing desert in the drought,
    A lake-land after rain;
To the skyline sweeps the waving grass,
    Or whirls the scorching sand—
A phantom land, a mystic realm!
    The Never-Never Land.

Where lone Mount Desolation lies,
    Mounts Dreadful and Despair,
'Tis lost beneath the rainless skies
    In hopeless deserts there;
It spreads nor'-west by No-Man's-Land—
    Where clouds are seldom seen—
To where the cattle-stations lie
    Three hundred miles between.

THE NEVER-NEVER LAND

The drovers of the Great Stock Routes
  The strange Gulf Country know,
Where, travelling for the northern grass,
  The big lean bullocks go;
And camped by night where plains lie wide,
  Like some old ocean's bed,
The stockmen in the starlight ride
  Round fifteen hundred head.

And west of named and numbered days
  The shearers walk and ride,
Jack Cornstalk and the Ne'er-do-well
  And Greybeard side by side;
They veil their eyes from moon and stars,
  And slumber on the sand—
Sad memories sleep as years go round
  In Never-Never Land.

O rebels to society!
  The Outcasts of the West—
O hopeless eyes that smile for me,
  And broken hearts that jest!
The pluck to face a thousand miles,
  The grit to see it through!
The Communism perfected
  Till man to man is True!

The Arab to the desert sand,
  The Finn to fens and snow,
The "Flax-stick" dreams of Maoriland,
  While seasons come and go.
Whatever stars may glow or burn
  O'er lands of East and West,
The wandering heart of man will turn
  To one it loves the best.

Lest in the city I forget
   True mateship, after all,
My water-bag and billy yet
   Are hanging on the wall.
And I, to save my soul, again
   Would tramp to sunsets grand
With sad-eyed mates across the plain
   In the Never-Never Land.

1902

After the War

THE big rough boys from the runs out back were first where the balls flew free,
And yelled in the slang of the Outside Track: "By God, it's a Christmas spree!"
"It's not too dusty"—and "Wool away!—stand clear o' the blazin' shoots!"
"Sheep O! Sheep O!"—"We'll cut out to-day"—"Look out for the boss's boots!"
"What price the tally in camp to-night!"—"What price the boys Out Back!"
"Go it, you tigers, for Right or Might and the pride of the Outside Track!"—
"Needle and thread!"—"I have broke my comb!"—"Now ride, you flour-bags, ride!"
"Fight for your mates and the folks at home!" "Here's one for the Lachlan-side!"
Those men of the West would sneer and scoff at the gates of hell ajar,
And often the sight of a head cut off was hailed by a yell for "Tar!"

.   .   .   .

I heard the Push in the Red Redoubt, grown wild at a luckless shot:
"Look out for the bloomin' shell, look out!"—"Gorblimy, but that's red-hot!"

"It's Bill the Slogger—poor bloke—he's done. A chunk of the shell was his;
I wish the beggar that fired that gun could get within reach of Liz."
"Those foreign gunners will give us rats, but I wish it was Bill they'd missed.
I'd like to get at their bleedin' hats with a rock in my (something) fist."

"Hold up, Billy; I'll stick to you; they've hit you under the belt.
If we get the waddle I'll swag you through, if the blazin' mountains melt;
You remember the night I was held by the traps for stoushing a bleedin' Chow,
And you went for 'em proper and laid out three, and I won't forget it now."
And, groaning and swearing, the pug replied: "I'm done . they've knocked me out!
I'd fight 'em all for a pound a side, from the boss to the rouseabout.
My nut is cracked and my legs is broke, and it gives me worse than hell;
I trained for a scrap with a twelve-stone bloke, and not with a bursting shell.
You needn't mag, for I knowed, old chum. I *knowed*, old pal, you'd stick;
But you can't hold out till the boys come up, and you'd best be nowhere quick.
They've got a force and a gun ashore, and both of our wings is broke;
They'll storm the ridge in a minute more, and the best you can do is 'smoke.'"

AFTER THE WAR

And Jim exclaimed: "You can smoke, you chaps, but me—Gor' bli' me, no!
The Push that ran from the George-street traps won't run from a foreign foe.
I'll stick to the gun while she makes them sick, and I'll stick to what's left of Bill."
And they hiss through their blackened teeth: "We'll stick! by the blazin' flame, we will!"
And long years after the war was past, they told in the town and bush
How the ridge of death to the bloody last was held by a Sydney push;
How they fought to the end in a sheet of flame, how they fought with their rifle-stocks,
And earned, in a nobler sense, the name of their ancient weapons —rocks.

.   .   .   .

In the Western camps it was ever our boast, when 'twas bad for the Kangaroo,
"If the enemy's forces take the coast, they must take the mountains, too;
They may force their way by the Western line or round by a northern track,
But they won't run short of a decent spree with the men who are left Out Back!"
When we burst the enemy's ironclads and won by a run of luck,
We whooped as loudly as Nelson's lads when a French three-decker struck;
And when the enemy's troops prevailed the truth was never heard—
We lied like heroes, and never failed to explain how that occurred.

You Bushmen sneer in the old bush way at the new-chum jackeroo,
But cuffs-'n'-collars were out that day, and they stuck to their posts like glue;
I never believed that a dude could fight till a Johnny led us then;
We buried his bits in the rear that night for the honour of Pitt-street men.
And Jim the Ringer—he fought, he did. The regiment nicknamed Jim
"Old Heads-a-Caser" and "Heads-a-Quid," but it never was tails with him.
The way that he rode was a racing rhyme, and the way that he finished grand;
He backed the enemy every time, and died in a hand-to-hand!

. . . .

I'll never forget when the Ringer and I were first in the Bush Brigade,
With Warrego Bill, from the Live-till-you-Die, in the last grand charge we made.
And Billy died—he was full of sand—he said, as I raised his head:
"I'm full of love for my native land, but a lot too full of lead.
Tell 'em," said Billy; "and tell old Dad to look after the cattle pup";
But his eyes grew bright, though his voice was sad, and he said, as I held him up:
"I have been happy on western farms. And once, when I first went wrong,
Around my neck were the trembling arms of the girl I'd loved so long.

AFTER THE WAR

Far out on the southern seas I've sailed; I've ridden where brumbies roam,
And often when all on the station failed I've driven the outlaw home.
I've spent a cheque in a day and night, and I've made a cheque as quick;
I've struck a nugget when times were tight and the stores had stopped our tick.
I've led the field on the old bay mare, and I hear the cheering still,
When mother and sister and *she* were there, and the old man yelled for Bill;
But, save for *her,* could I live my time again in the old Bush way,
I'd give it all for the last half-mile in the race we rode to-day!"
And he passed away as the stars came out—he died as old heroes die—
I heard the sound of the distant rout, and the Southern Cross was high.

1895

The Jolly Dead March

IF I ever be worthy or famous—
    Which I'm sadly beginning to doubt—
When the angel whose place 'tis to name us
    Shall say to my spirit, "Pass out!"
I wish for no sniv'lling about me
    (My work was the work of the land)
But I hope that my country will shout me
    The price of a decent brass band.

Oh, let it strike up "Annie Laurie,"
    And let it burst out with "Lang Syne"—
Twin voices of sadness and glory
    That have ever been likings of mine.
And give the French war-hymn deep-throated
    With "The Star Spangled Banner" between,
But let the last mile be devoted
    To "Britannia" and "Wearing the Green."

Thump! thump! of the drums and "Te-ri-rit,"
    Thump! thump! of the drum—'twill be grand,
Though only in dream or in spirit
    To ride or flit after that band!
While myself and my mourners go straying
    And strolling and drifting along,
With the cornets in front of us playing
    The tune of an old battle-song!

THE JOLLY DEAD MARCH

I ask for no "turn-out" to bear me;
   I ask not for railings or slabs,
And spare me, my country, oh, spare me
   The hearse and the long string of cabs!
And if, in the end—more's the pity—
   There's fame more than money to spare—
A vanman I know in the city
   Will cart me "This side up with care."

And my spirit will join the procession—
   Will pause, so to speak, on the brink—
Nor feel the least shade of depression
   When the mourners drop out for a drink;
It may be a hot day in December,
   Or a cold day in June it may be,
And a drink will but help them remember
   The good points the world missed in me.

"Unhook the West Port" for an orphan,
   An old digger chorus revive—
If you don't hear a whoop from the coffin,
   I am *not* being buried alive.
But I'll go with a spirit less bitter
   Than mine on this earth's ever been,
And, perhaps, to save trouble, Saint Peter
   Will pass me, two comrades between.

Thump! thump! of the drums we inherit—
   War-drums of my dreams—oh, it's grand!
Be this the reward of all merit
   To ride or march after a band!
As we, the World-Battlers, go straying
   And loving and laughing along—
With Hope in the lead of us playing
   The tune of a life-battle song!

Then let them strike up "Annie Laurie,"
   And let 'em burst out with "Lang Syne,"
Twin voices of sadness and glory
   That have ever been likings of mine.
Let them swell the French war-hymn deep-throated
   (And I'll not buck at "God Save the Queen")
But let the last mile be devoted
   To "Britannia" and "Wearing the Green."

1897

For'ard

I T is stuffy in the steerage where the second-classers sleep,
    For there's near a hundred for'ard, and they're stowed away like sheep—
    They are trav'lers for the most part in a straight 'n' honest path;
But their linen's rather scanty, an' there isn't any bath—
Stowed away like ewes and wethers that is shore 'n' marked 'n' draft;
But the shearers of the shearers always seem to travel aft—
    In the cushioned cabins, aft,
    With saloons 'n' smoke-rooms, aft—
There is sheets 'n' best of tucker for the first-salooners, aft.

Our beef is just like scrapin's from the inside of a hide,
And the spuds were pulled too early, for they're mostly green inside;
But from somewhere back amidships there's a smell o' cookin' waft,
An' I'd give my earthly prospects for a real good tuck-out aft—
    Ham an' eggs, 'n' coffee, aft,
    Say, cold fowl for luncheon, aft,
Juicy grills an' toast 'n' cutlets—tucker a-lor-frongsy, aft.

They feed our women sep'rate, an' they make a blessed fuss,
Just as if they couldn't trust 'em for to eat along with us!

Just because our hands are horny an' our hearts are rough with
    graft—
But the gentlemen and ladies always "dine" together aft—
        With their ferns an' mirrors, aft,
        With their flow'rs an' napkins, aft—
"I'll assist you to an orange"—"Kindly pass the sugar," aft.

We are shabby, rough, 'n' dirty, an' our feelin's out of tune,
An' it's hard on fellers for'ard that was used to go saloon;
There's a broken swell amongst us—he is barracked, he is chaffed,
An' I wish at times, poor devil, for his own sake he was aft;
        For they'd understand him, aft,
        (He will miss the bath-rooms aft)
Spite of all there's no denying that there's finer feelin's aft.

Last night we watched the moonlight as it spread across the sea—
"It is hard to make a livin'," said the broken swell to me,
"There is ups and downs," I answered, an' a bitter laugh he
    laughed—
There were brighter days an' better when he always travelled
    aft—
        With his rug an' gladstone, aft,
        With his cap an' spyglass, aft—
A careless, rovin', gay young spark as always travelled aft.

There's a notice by the gangway, an' it seems to come amiss,
For it says that second-classers ain't allowed abaft o' this;
An' there ought to be a notice for the fellows from abaft—
But the smell an' dirt's a warnin' to the first-salooners, aft;
        With their tooth and nail-brush, aft,
        With their cuffs an' collars, aft—
Their cigars an' books, an' papers, an' their cap-peaks fore-'n'-aft.

I want to breathe the mornin' breeze that blows against the boat,
For there's a swellin' in my heart, a tightness in my throat.
We are for'ard when there's trouble! We are for'ard when
 there's graft!
But the men who never battle always seem to travel aft;
        With their dressin'-cases, aft,
        With their swell pyjamas, aft—
Yes! the idle and the careless, they have ease an' comfort aft.

I feel so low an' wretched, as I mooch about the deck,
That I'm ripe for jumpin' over—an' I wish there was a wreck!
We are driven to New Zealand to be shot out over there,
Scarce a shillin' in our pockets, nor a decent rag to wear,
With the everlastin' worry lest we don't get into graft—
Oh, there's little left to land for if you cannot travel aft.
        No anxiety abaft,
        They have stuff to land with, aft—
There is little left to land for if you cannot travel aft.

But it's grand at sea this mornin', an' Creation almost speaks,
Sailin' past the Bay of Islands with its pinnacles an' peaks,
With the sunny haze all round us an' the white-caps on the blue,
An' the orphan rocks an' breakers—oh, it's glorious sailin'
 through!
To the south a distant steamer, to the west a coastin' craft,
An' we see the beauty for'ard—can they see it better aft?—
        Spite of op'ra-glasses, aft;
        But, ah well, they're brothers aft—
Nature seems to draw us closer—bring us nearer fore-'n'-aft.

What's the use of bein' bitter? What's the use of gettin' mad?
What's the use of bein' narrer just because yer luck is bad?
What's the blessed use of frettin' like a child that wants the moon?
There is broken hearts an' trouble in the gilded First Saloon!

We are used to bein' shabby—we have got no overdraft—
We can laugh at troubles for'ard that they couldn't laugh at aft!
   Spite o' pride an' tone abaft
   (Keepin' up appearance, aft)
There's anxiety an' worry in the breezy cabins aft.

But the curse of class distinctions from our shoulders shall be hurled,
An' the sense of Human Kinship revolutionize the world;
There'll be higher education for the toilin' starvin' clown,
An' the rich an' educated shall be educated down;
Then we all will meet amidships on this stout old earthly craft,
An' there won't be any friction 'twixt the classes fore-'n'-aft.
   We'll be brothers, fore-'n'-aft!
   Yes, an' sisters, fore-'n'-aft!
When the people work together, and there ain't no fore-'n'-aft.

1893

W. C. Penfold & Co. Ltd., Printers, 183 Pitt Street, Sydney.

ImTheStory.com

Personalized Classic Books in many genre's

Unique gift for kids, partners, friends, colleagues

Customize:

- Character Names
- Upload your own front/back cover images (optional)
- Inscribe a personal message/dedication on the inside page (optional)

Customize many titles Including
- Alice in Wonderland
- Romeo and Juliet
- The Wizard of Oz
- A Christmas Carol
- Dracula
- Dr. Jekyll & Mr. Hyde
- And more...

Emily's Adventures in Wonderland

Ryan & Julia